SURVIVAL OF THE AMERICAN PEOPLE

SURVIVAL
OF THE
AMERICAN PEOPLE

JULIUS SENTONGO

Tate Publishing & *Enterprises*

Survival of the American People

Published by Tate Publishing & Enterprises, LLC
127 E. Trade Center Terrace | Mustang, Oklahoma 73064 USA
1.888.361.9473 | www.tatepublishing.com

Tate Publishing is committed to excellence in the publishing industry. The company reflects the philosophy established by the founders, based on Psalm 68:11,
"The Lord gave the word and great was the company of those who published it."

Cover design by Sarah Kirchen
Interior design by Christina Hicks

Published in the United States of America

ISBN: 978-1-61777-611-3
1. Religion / Religion, Politics & State
2. Religion / Christian Life / Social Issures
11.05.17

DEDICATION

To our lovely mum, Gloria Kiggundu. Thank you for believing God that this book would make such a big impact on lives. Thanks for being a caring and loving mum. Thanks for your prayers and support. Thanks for accepting Jesus Christ. This unites us more here on earth and in heaven forevermore if our focus remains meeting Jesus Christ.

You are a true mother who loves and desires to see the unity of our family with our dad, Fred Kiggundu, who went to be with the LORD and his waiting to meet with us in heaven.

God bless you, all the days of your life.

ACKNOWLEDGMENTS

This book wouldn't have been possible without the support of my dear mother, Gloria Nanono Kiggundu, and my siblings, Dan and Florah.

Thanks also go to our pastor, Samuel Kawumi, for his knowledgeable support throughout the years, and all the disciples of Jesus Christ at Blessed Christian Church Mukono in Uganda. Thanks to my sister, Anet Nalumansi, who typed the message.

Thanks to all of you that are praying salvation for the American people.

Thanks also to the staff at Tate Publishing and Enterprises for making this project possible.

I thank God for his forgiveness and healing of hearts that come with this message.

God loves you, and Jesus Christ is Lord.

TABLE OF CONTENTS

America's Forefathers And
Their Christian Legacy 11

America's Current State 33

The Purpose Of God's Leading America 61

The State Of America's Family 85

The State Of America's
Education System 111

The Devil's Plan 127

The State Of The American Individual 141

The Future Of America 181

Endnotes 201

AMERICA'S FOREFATHERS AND THEIR CHRISTIAN LEGACY

America is one of the countries in the world that was founded, formed, and today exists by faith in the Word of God. This is largely from what governs America as a nation, and looking at the spirit with which the country was formed entirely basing everything on the Bible, which is the Word of God. Just like America, Israel too exists by faith as seen from the Holy Scriptures, the Bible, understanding that its formation was a work of faith, when Abraham was promised by God that he would one day have descendants as many as the stars of the sky (Genesis 15:5 NKJV). Then He brought him outside and said, "Look now toward heaven, and count the stars if you are able to number them." And He said to him, "So shall your descendants be." The promise of God to Abraham was fulfilled as the whole story unfolds resulting into a nation Israel. This is easy to believe, because this is written in the Bible. What is not straightforward is how America was formed by faith on the Word of God. We ask ourselves how this happened. Only be patient and follow through the entire message, because we can't comprehend this revelation with our natural mind. Only by the help of God shall we be able to understand how it happened and why this is important to understand.

The God of Israel is the God of the Bible revealing Himself in different ways for different purposes, yet He is the same God. Surely God is all that He says He is, as God the father, God the Son, God the Holy Spirit; also, He's the everlasting God. He is the God of promise, called the God of covenant; the true, living, merciful and just God, the God of Abraham, Isaac, and Jacob, more over the God who loves all men and women on earth as with all his creation.

As God, He chose Israel that they would make Him known to the whole world as the only true God and God of all creation.

In those days the people didn't recognize Him as a living God, they imagined God was the things that looked supernatural, for example, the moon and the stars, the mountains, and many more. By this they did all sorts of evil before Him their creator as forms of worship, yet He desires one thing called obedience and love.

For Him to show himself, God chooses Abraham to become Israel with plans of getting the whole world to know and understand that He is their creator. He wanted them to put their trust in Him; He wanted people to relate with Him as their friend and God and to live just as He created them to live. To God, this is the most important. For example, He gives life, yet without the knowledge of this truth, we forget that life is today and tomorrow may be not, so we end up living a life full of misery, yet life should be lived in its fullness and in honor of God who gives it. This is why God proved himself in all that He says He is and much more when He walked with the children of Israel, doing all that He did for them. God is not partial but open to becoming the God of all that believe in Him. He's the God of promise, He is faithful to His Word and He says, "Seek me and you will find me." This is to all that will seek Him for this has been the case from then to this day.

Israel became the People of God as it is to this day. He is God; He chose them. God explains what happened and what will happen through Paul's message to the Gentiles. "Gentiles; inasmuch as I am an apostle to the Gentiles, I magnify my ministry, if by any means I may provoke to jealousy those who are my flesh and save some of them. For if their being cast away is the reconciling of the world, what will their acceptance be but life from the dead?

For if the first fruit is holy, the lump is also holy; and if the root is holy, so are the branches. And if some of the branches were broken off, and you, being a wild olive tree, were grafted in among them, and with them became a partaker of the root and fatness of the olive tree, do not boast against the branches. But if you do boast, remember that you do not support the root, but the root supports you.

You will say then, "Branches were broken off that I might be grafted in." Well said. Because of unbelief they were broken off, and you stand by faith. Do not be haughty, but fear. For if God did not spare the natural branches, He may not spare you either.

Therefore consider the goodness and severity of God: on those who fell, severity; but toward you, goodness, if you continue in His goodness. Otherwise you also will be cut off. And they also, if they do not continue in unbelief, will be grafted in, for God is able to graft them in again. For I do not desire, brethren, that you should be ignorant of this mystery, lest you should be wise in your own opinion, that blindness in part has happened to Israel until the fullness of the Gentiles has come in. And so all Israel will be saved,[g] as it is written: " The Deliverer will come out of Zion, And He will turn away ungodliness from Jacob; For this is My covenant with them, When I take away their sins." (Romans 11: 13-24 NKJV) The Word of God is talking about Israel; some haven't accepted Jesus Christ but also says the time is coming when we shall have no grace to salvation as gentiles so that they (Israel) the natural branches will be grafted in "that blindness in part has happened to Israel until the fullness of the Gentiles has come in. And so all Israel will be saved" Before that time comes which is not far from happening, God warns us from boasting against Israel, the branch, because Israel will be saved, their time began already and many have individually began to accept Jesus as their brother but importantly as their personal LORD and savior.

Today grace exists to people of the whole earth to all countries and tribes, all to believe in Jesus, grafted in as wild olive tree like the scripture explains. The Bible further explains about us when we choose to follow Jesus that we become sons of God what a privilege we have; "He was in the world, and the world was made through Him, and the world did not know Him. He came to His own, [c] and His own [d] did not receive Him. But as many as received Him, to them He gave the right to become children of God, to those who believe in His name: who were born, not of blood, nor of the will of the flesh, nor of the will of man, but of God". (John 1:12-13 NKJV)

So what brings in America to be a people of God or what makes America to be founded in faith was that the American Forefathers chose the same God, the God of Israel. Though they practiced different religions, they had one thing in common. This was their faith in the living God. Some of the forefathers doubted the power of the Bible. This didn't stop the plan of God for the ones that were fully committed to believing every beat of it, because they all looked for a free land. Is God partial? The same thing happened to some of the children of Israel who doubted the promises of God for a promised land at some point; this didn't mean they didn't know who God was.

When we study what the forefathers always said and did at different occasions in different times, we shall notice that they were always bearing witness for their faith in God. What they did was an inspiration of the Holy Spirit. This very one reason of acknowledging Him as God and believing in His son Jesus Christ is just good and can be the beginning of a relationship with Him, we shall look at several founding fathers confessions throughout the message, let's first look at one of them.

Thomas Jefferson known for all his accomplishments, his words will bring light to this revelation of America being founded on faith in God. As a forefather he said, "God who gave us life gave us liberty. And can the liberties of a nation be thought secure when we have removed their only firm basis, a conviction in the minds of the people that these liberties are a gift from God? That they are not to be violated but with His wrath? Indeed

I tremble for my country when I reflect that God is just, and that His justice cannot sleep forever."[1]

Such acknowledgement of God was not ignored by God, so that He looked at the forefathers and honored their plans just as He honored the promise He made to Abraham, giving him descendants, the children of Israel. God further promised Abraham that through him all the world was to be blessed this was fulfilled and is true when Jesus Christ the savior was born from Abraham's descendants.

> I will bless those who bless you,
> And I will curse him who curses you;
> And in you all the families of the earth shall be blessed."
>
> Genesis 12:3 (KJV)

God loves obedience. He was moved by the obedience of the forefathers as He was moved by the obedience of Abraham. It was all about a people who loved him and hated evil; such were the reasons for Israel's greatness in the times of Moses and Joshua. So for their obedience, God did the same thing for the forefathers during the founding of America, as His Word was to the children of Israel crossing from Egypt to their promised land.

America's forefathers knew God through the Bible as the only giver of liberty, prosperity, peace; minus Him, the nation couldn't make it. So as leaders they had a responsibility of protecting the people they led. They did this through warning the inhabitants every time through communications like letters, but also by speaking about Jesus Christ and his teachings and explaining the beauty of Christian values as their personal source of inspirations, power, strength, and encouragement. This they did always when they had the opportunity.

Patrick Henry had this revelation:

> It cannot be emphasized too clearly and too often that this nation was founded, not by religionists, but by Christians; not on religion, but on the gospel of Jesus Christ. For this very reason, peoples of other faiths have been afforded asylum, prosperity, and freedom of worship here.[2]

Patrick Henry answers our question of whether our country America was founded on Christian values. He is being informative about what could be a question to us today. We can connect both statements the one by Thomas Jefferson and the one by Patrick Henry both speaking of Christianity and the role God and his Word played in the founding of America. America is a country founded on biblical truth, founded by believers this is what America is all about just as we shall continue to discover. Part of what we have looked at so far has been in the formation of the nation. Looking at how America was founded by faith in God. Some of this and more can be found in several books about the founding of America as a nation written as part of history documented about the country.

The forefathers speak of God in their times but what happened before them? Understanding these largely undocumented events through God telling us what happened before will help us find out why the forefathers spoke about past times in their present times. Patrick Henry's will talks about the past tense "this nation was founded" which could be just before that time but could also be so many years back before that time he made his will in.

Several hundred years ago, different people left their motherlands in Europe to look for a land where they would serve God and worship him with sincere and truthful spirits without boundaries. They pleased God in their plans, so God fulfilled their dreams. It was hard and painful, yet several people today all over the world are blessed because of these men's visions.

Up to this day, these men are still honored for their bravery, love for God, their faith, and their fear of God. America has known them through leaders, through songs, through stories, and these men are the forefathers of the America we are talking about.

William Bradford one of the forefathers wrote that they [the Pilgrims] were seeking "A better and easier place of living, a great hope, and for the propagating and advancing the gospel of the kingdom of Christ in those remote parts of the world." [3]

William Bradford Spoke just as the Bible talks about Abraham in Hebrews:

> By faith Abraham, when he was called to go out into a place which he should after receive for an inheritance, obeyed; and he went

> out, not knowing whither he went. By faith he sojourned in the land of promise, as in a strange country, dwelling in tabernacles with Isaac and Jacob, the heirs with him of the same promise for he looked for a city which hath foundations, whose builder and maker is God.
>
> Hebrews 10: 8-10 (KJV)

What is important to note is the way the Bible explains about Abraham's faith. It says, "by faith Abraham," and this is the same faith that was exercised by the forefathers, because by "faith" the forefathers sojourned in the land of promise as in a strange country; for they also looked for a city which had its foundations, whose builder and maker was God."

The forefathers, having lived in bondage before they came to America as their promised land, believed God for a land as was promised to the children of Israel a "free land." We remember that the children of Israel's reason for leaving Egypt, led by Moses, was that they would go to a far land to freely worship and serve God.

Then the revelation and connection is that these two events or scenarios are similar: the children of Israel's leaving Egypt, a place of bondage, to a free land flowing with milk and honey, and the forefathers' journey from Europe, which was then a place of bondage, to a free land flowing with milk and honey, their promised land, the present America.

This is why Israel is similar to America as we have seen above and as we shall continue to note. This is very important to be clearly understood, because some specific things that happened to the children of Israel happened to the American forefathers, and other similar circumstances might continue happening to both countries.

The revelation is that the future of America should not be such a secret; we shall look at the children of Israel warned by God about being disobedient, and this will help us to learn what can happen to America if we chose obedience or disobedience against God.

We have looked at both nations' formations as based on the word of God and have also just looked at both nations' similar events before America became a nation.

Note that this is why the devil has continually challenged both nations' peace, which only springs from the obedience to worship the ruler of peace, Jesus Christ, as LORD and Savior. When, both Israel and America, deviates from this truth, we are lost and losing our peace with us.

Please remember, America, that the Word of God is active and lives. God will use the same word to speak to us today, just as he used it to speak to the children of Israel, which same word was believed by our forefathers years ago.

To the matters concerning the Promised Land, God told the children of Israel these words:

> Now, Israel, listen to the statutes and the judgments which I teach you to observe that you may live and go in and possess the land which the LORD God of your fathers is giving you. You shall not add to the word which I command you, nor take anything from it that you may keep the commandments of the LORD your God which I commend you.
>
> Deuteronomy 4:1(KJV)

And by faith, America's forefathers believed God through the same words. God was speaking to them to observe every statute so that they might live and go in and possess the land.

God, interestingly, says that even to go in and possess the land you have to live first before you possess the land, because the dead can't possess land, and we know that the "living" God talks about is a result of obedience to observe his commandments.

They understood that, yes, the land "America" could be possessed, but that living in the land would require obedience to God. And this is what America has missed today as a nation: the "obedience" to God which is essential to living in the present land "America."

The forefathers of America believed God for a promised land like the one God promised to the children of Israel, and, being that they chose God, God couldn't let them down. He fulfilled their desire and answered their prayers resulting to the glory seen today.

What happened after that was dependent on an individual basis, some terrible things happened which were not appropriate, and this has been recognized and dealt with accordingly.

They believed in the caution not to be disobedient to God by walking in their own ways which are ways of the tempter Satan (devil). This was done to avoid angering God when they kept the concise of repentance of sin. They instead pleased God. This explains why the Word of God was of such value in America during those days more so than today.

To this day, America is the dream country to all. Those who have gone out of America, visiting other countries, will agree with the truth that America flows with milk and honey. Although the flowing today can't be compared to the flowing some years back in different ways, it still flows with milk and honey just as the faith of the forefathers was.

We thank the Lord our God for the forefathers who lived selflessly and that today success has been greatly achieved. On the other side, one wonders why this courage lacks today, forgetting the things that make for our peace.

We have neglected who they were, and we shall agree that the outcomes have been unbearable. Without repentance, this can be just the beginning of a great cost. Such is what the devil has planned for us individually and as a country.

God is reminding us not to leave his statutes, laws, and commandments; not to follow other foreign gods that will cause a shortening of our days in this Promised Land, "America"; a fulfilled dream of the forefathers.

The forefathers believed in the LORD Jesus Christ who gave them the victory. America then became a great and prosperous land, because they chose to worship Jesus Christ, the Prince of Peace. The peace they had was the beginning of all things, without which nothing was accomplished that has been accomplished.

The three branches of the US government—judicial, legislative, and executive—were proposed by James Madison, who was the fourth president of the United States. He proposed the plan to divide the central government into three branches. He discovered this model of government from the "Perfect Governor" as he read Isaiah 33:22: "For the LORD is our judge, the LORD is our lawgiver, the LORD is our king; He will save us." [4]

This inspiration from God's Word was adopted by Madison and has been a basis for all the victories America has claimed. These victories have also been claimed by many nations around the world who have adopted America's model. God builds nations; without God, anything can be compromised and any trouble can befall any individual or nation regardless of greatness, because the greatness and wisdom are not by man but from God.

It's that understanding in God that was expressed by the forefathers that made America the light of the world to this day.

"A city that is set on a hill cannot be hidden nor do they light a lamp and put it under a basket but on a lamp stand, and it gives light to all who are in the house" (Matthew 5:14, NKJV).

Jesus Christ teaches this truth when talking about how a changed person should live. He says everyone around this person shall see their light. The light of the forefathers brought glory to the country, and who doesn't know America to this day? This is like what we talked about when explaining why God chose Israel; he simply wanted others to learn about Him through Israel.

And what we see is that the forefathers decided to be chosen, too, when they decided to follow Jesus Christ and worship the true God. God knew America would wisely and faithfully use its influence and power as a land of believers to be an example to the world, showing how God is to be worshiped and obeyed through His Word the Bible.

As American people we are the Light of the world but where is our light as a Nation? Where is our light individually? Being that we are the Christians, God is asking us and wants to know.

The American people that protected God's law have now gone against the law.

Deciding to choose rights that lead us to disobeying the ways of God and live just a short time, desiring to please men rather than pleasing their creator? Could it also be that our love is getting cold? These days being last days, do we recognize these times? How could we recognize the times if the Bible doesn't have any meaning to us as a nation any more than it did with the times of the forefathers? Please remember that "pride goes before destruction and a haughty spirit before a fall" (Proverbs 16:18 NKJV).

If the forefathers came back today, would they see Americans as faithful or they would see us as a disobedient people, a people that have not known the times but have also deliberately not read their history to find out why their land survived? And this has left God wondering how far we are likely to go if we disregard him this much.

What would the forefathers say about the present day America where God has been shifted from His place and what could the forefathers have done since, we honor them today. Should we imagine their times were easier than our times? To be true they had worse times, but made choices better than us the inhabitants of the Land today.

To the forefathers making choices depended on what was good before God, this was very important, and this made all the difference. How are we making decisions today? So many good things just as mentioned before came simply from this understanding of making choices depending on what God's Word says is pure.

If the laws, the commandments, are to be forgotten by the American people, or if something is added to the Word of God, what will the world think we have become?

God is saying that obedience to him is a blessing, and surely America will stay a great nation; a wise and understanding people if we choose obedience just as the forefathers did.

But what are we doing about it? When we have continued to underplay the source of God's assistance, which is his Word, deciding that the Bible should not be taught to our children in schools. We ought to remember God works through his Word only; no other way.

America was a land that honoured God, a land that truthfully worshipped God. But we shall agree that so much has changed in America today. In these days, people are no longer hungry for the truth. The neglect to do what pleases God first to what pleases us has devoured us and this is not what the forefathers dreamt about. Freedom was their dream since their coming from Europe, and when freedom dies, and then we become slaves to an invisible master called sin. When this master (sin) is in charge of us, our freedom is a professed freedom, not the true freedom anymore. Jesus Christ explains this issue so well.

Jesus said, "Most assuredly, I say to you, whoever commits sin is a slave of sin" (John 8:34, KJV).

Jesus Christ shows us that when we commit sin we are no longer free but have become slaves to sin. We ask ourselves what sins we have committed. God is not the judge, but just as Jesus Christ explained, the word we know judges us. Thanks to God, we shall see how we can be set free from this sinful life in the following chapters.

The forefathers' obedience and trust in God meant everything to them, so Benjamin Franklin asked,

> In the beginning of the contest with Britain, when we were sensible of danger, we had daily prayers in this room for Divine protection. Our prayers, Sir, were heard, and they were graciously answered… do we imagine we no longer need His assistance? [5]

He posed that question which can still be asked today. Do we imagine we no longer need his assistance?

AMERICA'S CURRENT STATE

Who saw the glory of America during the times of the forefathers? Who has read about how the people made decisions based on what their faith accepted only? Who was there to tell us what we should think America was then? Today we say that things must always change, not considering whether they should change for the good or worse. What main things have changed today about America? What has changed for the bad and what about those things that have changed for the good? All the above questions are subjective and could lead to different answers depending on who is answering and their present intentions. Thanks to God, we can find out answers ourselves.

How can we notice any change if we are not going to understand the past from the present. This can turn out to be just impossible. From the previous chapter we looked at the words of the forefathers, God uses them as no doubtable proof for explaining the change today. We didn't look at all of them but a few, especially considering leaders. We considered leaders, because leaders are a representative of the people they lead, although this is not always the case. Leaders to be elected should have shared values with the majority of the ones they lead. This is why our consideration of leaders to represent the ones they lead is not a bad idea.

By going back to the past we shall be able to discover the present changes. We shall look at what happened in the past, considering what the forefathers believed and why we should believe we are different from them today.

When the children of Israel in the Bible were being prepared to enter a land promised to them as descendants of Abraham, God, through Moses, spoke encouraging words to them, telling them that they were able to enter and possess the land, noticing that the same God who encouraged them also warned them to do all that he had commanded. The forefathers believed the same Word of God, and the promises of God in it and the warnings too.

Moses said,

> Therefore you shall be careful to do as the LORD God has commanded you. You shall not turn a side to the right hand or to the left. You shall walk in all the ways which the LORD your God has commanded you, that you may live and that it may be well with you, and that you may prolong your days in the land which you shall possess.
>
> Deuteronomy 5:32 (KJV)

Because God is just and the same God for all that believe in him through his Word, these words told to the children of Israel were the exact same words that the forefathers believed to have the same results as the children of Israel.

The forefathers knew that the land they were to possess was their promised land and chose to be careful. Careful to do as God had commanded in his Word. They didn't turn a side to the right hand or to the left. This was evident in the way they were consumed by God's Word, to the extent of proclaiming him faithful every time they had opportunity.

They continued to walk in all his ways. Note here the scripture says, "Shall be careful." "Shall" is an ongoing aspect, showing that it's done not once but continually.

The only reason the forefathers fled from their motherlands to the present America was because they hadn't been allowed the freedom to serve God as the word showed and taught them. With this zeal to serve God they crossed to America.

Thomas Jefferson said:

> The doctrines of Jesus are simple, and tend to all the happiness of man.
>
> Of all the systems of morality, ancient or modern, which have come under my observation, none appears to me so pure as that of Jesus.

He continued to say: "I am a real Christian, that is to say, a disciple of the doctrines of Jesus."

Thomas Jefferson expresses his love and conviction in the teaching of Jesus Christ to the extent of referring to himself as a disciple of Jesus

Christ. This is why we can agree about how they were consumed to worshiping God just as the Word taught and showed them.

To be a disciple means doing the Word of God, and Jesus Christ teaches about what it means to be a follower and a disciple when He said to the Jews who believed Him, "If you abide in my word, then you are my Disciples indeed" (John 8:31, KJV).

This is why abiding in Jesus Christ goes beyond saying we are Christians. Christianity is our way of life and all our actions. It's not the mere confession without the works of faith that affirms with this confession. "The disciples were called Christians first at Antioch" because their actions were just like the actions of Jesus Christ (Acts 11:26). Doing what Jesus did before he went to heaven, this is who Christians are. Are we anymore? We are not if we don't practice the works of Jesus Christ.

So God knew that we could meet in church buildings, homes, synagogues, or any other place to learn more about our Christian walk, but do we go to church anymore? We are feasting, or shopping as the ministers of the Word of God wait for us to attend services but don't see us. This has led to church buildings closing and some to be turned into warehouses.

Those empty churches today were built some years ago to accommodate a moderate population, yet as our population has increased, attendance in church has reduced. How are we preparing ourselves for our service before God, which is worshiping through our daily actions, if we no long meet to encourage each other as we fellowship? Like the first church did, meeting together was important and a basis for their success. If we have two events one about God and the other about something different what will our choice be? God knows our responses which would speak about our love we have for God today.

> Every day they continued to meet together in the temple courts. They broke bread in their homes and ate together with glad and sincere hearts, praising God and enjoying the favour of all the people. And the LORD added to their number daily those who were being saved.
>
> Acts 2:46-47 (NKJV)

We know that families that pray together, stay together, as do people who live in peace and freedom pray together; this is true love and expression of our freedom before God.

Today many Americans have mainly quoted one thing that came about by the forefathers, this is freedom. We say they made a way for freedom, forgetting to seek how this was possible. It was because the words of Jesus Christ abided richly in them. God is speaking to us, the American people; please seek him, the giver of freedom because, no man, no system, no security, no riches, and no anything can give freedom. Only God gives freedom and only through Jesus Christ can someone be free.

Jesus Christ gives freedom and freedom comes first individually and if the individuals have received personal freedom then the whole nation will be free. When we think we have freedom without individual freedom from Jesus Christ, the devil will prove us wrong, because he knows that individual freedom comes before national freedom. If the taker of freedom, who is Satan, the devil, wants to take freedom from a nation, like he has done today in America, he will attack individual freedom first, which causes blindness of individuals. This individual blindness is when an individual will not acknowledge sin in his life.

If this individual is blind, he will be used by the devil to spread his blindness. When this happens, all of a sudden everyone will end up with blindness. This is a blindness of the spirit, not physical blindness, and it is blindness to what is not right before God. People will do things they once couldn't imagine doing. In all this time, they don't even notice any wrong doing. Sometimes they get sympathy from men and support from the ones who don't do what they do which they use to justify their actions. To God this is where their freedom has been snatched from them. They, of course, think they have freedom but have lost it, just like that.

Freedom is a gift from God. Only God through his son Jesus Christ can give freedom.

Freedom as we have know can be in different forms as it's told to us, where it can be freedom of speech, freedom to exercise one's rights and many more forms of freedom; these are types of freedom yet limited to that particular subject. For example, we can have the right to say anything and everything we desire to speak, good or bad, useful or useless, this is the freedom of speech.

The kind of freedom that was given by God to the American forefathers was the freedom from sin, which is only given through faith in the LORD Jesus Christ and obedience to live as he says we should live.

If all the people are free, why should we need the freedom of speech? Why should people be stopped from speaking? Do we notice that sin causes the loss of freedom to speak, because someone is not doing what's right and is afraid of being exposed or talked about, so that the ones that want to speak about him need freedom to speak about what he is doing? Today's freedom is a different freedom from what was meant for the believed promised land of America, a land free from sin. Then freedom of speech was not necessary, because no one was afraid of being exposed so that he stopped people from speaking about what he did. Yet today this freedom has been taken away from us, the American people, by Satan. Yes, God is saying we have given away our freedom to the devil, that he torments us in what seems pleasure yet leads to destruction.

Benjamin Franklin, a forefather, also said:

> God governs in the affairs of man. And if a sparrow cannot fall to the ground without his notice, is it probable that an empire can rise without His aid? We have been assured in the Sacred Writings that except the LORD build the house, they labor in vain that build it. I firmly believe this. I also believe that, without His concurring aid, we shall not succeed in this political building no better than the builders of Babel. [6]

He spoke to inform the ones that were present and the ones in the future who will seek what caused the greatness. Are we building today, but without the head builder, the LORD Jesus? Then it must not be very hard for us to realize that if He, the LORD, is not helping in the building, then we are no different from the builders of the tower of Babel. It failed to be exact.

The difference in the forefathers and us today's inhabitants is that they walked by their words. In other words, they were as good as what they said. We only speak about God to please our neighbors or even to justify our actions. God sees this and is not pleased by what He sees.

John Adams continues,

> The general principles upon which the Fathers achieved independence were the general principals of Christianity....I will avow that I believed and now believe that those general principles of Christianity are as eternal and immutable as the existence and attributes of God. So July 4 ought to be commemorated as the day of deliverance by solemn acts of devotion to God Almighty. [7]

Surely from the above statements made by John Adams we can't doubt they purposed in their hearts to follow God through their faith in Jesus Christ, insofar as the Fourth of July was to be attributed to God. Does this day still exist? What can stop us from this day being a day attributed to God today? God waits for such to happen in this land again. After all, it's God who did everything that we enjoy today. This will be useful to help the new generation understand something about the forefathers that has been neglected for a long time. If we keep the youth ignorant about how this land is about God and not about what they have known it is about, we have no country. The plan of the devil is to destroy them with out their notice.

Yet today we have the separation of Church and state clause, which can stop this from happening. We can see how cunning the devil is that he knew such good things would happen and to stop such from happening a law is in place today, supported by ourselves.

The questions to ask ourselves about this clause are: What was its cause back then? How beneficial has it been to God? Could it be that we want this clause out of fear and uncertainty of who will be in office and what they will do? What about if we are just selfish about denying help from whoever could benefit from the support of government? If they benefitted, is it to the glory of God, or is it about our camp having lost to them so they are benefitting. We must make sure this is not about us, us disagreeing about very simple things like, "Who knows God more than the other? Who is true and who is lying about their practices? Who has the biggest number of followers than the other? Whose religion is more popular than the other? Who started his church first than the other?" We forget that the kingdom of God and this world is not about who is best and who is smarter.

The motive behind all we do can be hidden from the people and the country we serve but can't be hidden from God. This is how by ourselves the freedom we wanted to achieve and protect can slowly begin to leave the land. Let us imagine: Two people among us disagree on a small thing; no council is given to them from God's Word, and the next thing happening is a law in place. Is this the way we have chosen to go?

Of course, the separation of state and church helped to solve the problem of the two and solved the problem of a church (state) that imposed its law forcefully on the people in those days. With all the good we attach to the clause, this clause has been a very big hindrance to the kingdom of God in many ways. We protected ourselves, yes, but God has not benefitted; instead a cunning devil has used the loophole to block every good that would come from the Word of God.

It's good to remember that before the children of Israel kings came into existence in the times of the children of Israel, God had leaders from Moses to Samuel who could be a symbol of government today, and, at the same time, these leaders showed the children of Israel how to love God as their responsibility; we can refer to this duty as a symbol of church today. From this we see faithful servants of God being (state) government and church joined. This doesn't sound like separation of church and state. From that we remember the idea of kings who make and have governments wasn't from God, nor is the issue of separation of church and state. Such happened because of our heart hardening.

> Now it came to pass when Samuel was old that he made his sons judges over Israel. The name of his firstborn was Joel, and the name of his second, Abijah; they were judges in Beersheba. But his sons did not walk in his ways; they turned aside after dishonest gain, took bribes, and perverted justice.

Then all the elders of Israel gathered together and came to Samuel at Ramah, and said to him, "Look, you are old, and your sons do not walk in your ways. Now make us a king to judge us like all the nations."

But the thing displeased Samuel when they said, "Give us a king to judge us." So Samuel prayed to the LORD. And the LORD said to Samuel, "Heed the voice of the people in all that they say to you; for they have not rejected you, but they have rejected Me, that I should not reign over them. According to all the works which they have done since the day that I brought them up out of Egypt, even to this day—with which they have forsaken Me and served other gods—so they are doing to you also. Now therefore, heed their voice. However, you shall solemnly forewarn them, and show them the behaviour of the king who will reign over them."

So Samuel told all the words of the LORD to the people who asked him for a king. And he said, "This will be the behaviour of the king who will reign over you: He will take your sons and appoint them for his own chariots and to be his horsemen, and some will run before his chariots. He will appoint captains over his thousands and captains over his fifties, will set some to plow his ground and reap his harvest, and some to make his weapons of war and equipment for his chariots. He will take your daughters to be perfumers, cooks, and bakers. And he will take the best of your fields, your vineyards, and your olive groves, and give them to his servants. He will take a tenth of your grain and your vintage, and give it to his officers and servants. And he will take your male servants, your female servants, your finest young men, [a] and your donkeys, and put them to his work. He will take a tenth of your sheep.

> And you will be his servants. And you will cry out in that day because of your king whom you have chosen for yourselves, and the LORD will not hear you in that day."
>
> Nevertheless the people refused to obey the voice of Samuel; and they said, "No, but we will have a king over us, that we also may be like all the nations, and that our king may judge us and go out before us and fight our battles."
>
> And Samuel heard all the words of the people, and he repeated them in the hearing of the LORD. So the LORD said to Samuel, "Heed their voice, and make them a king."
>
> And Samuel said to the men of Israel, "Every man go to his city."
>
> 1 Samuel 18:1-22 NKJV

What happened in the scriptures above helps us to see what we sometimes do today and say, if it is happening today, and then God is fine with it and behind it. Many times he is not.

We know that there were many troubles that caused Thomas Jefferson's letter about the separation of Church and State. Who knew if the church and state could become like what happened in Europe back then? So he suggested this proposal. Today is different; can't we trust them? If we can't trust them, we must begin working towards those times when we shall be able to trust their judgements about the things of God. These people are from our communities, we go to the same churches with them, go to the same schools with them; they are dads and mums, grandmothers; why can't we trust their judgement about the things of God? What about if they have limits and become accountable of their actions on this exact subject, can this be better than totally blocking every plan of God in the name of the first Amendment right?

We could also reason that not every one of us practices the same religion, or even some of us don't believe in God, and we know it's their freedom to make that decision. Are we sure they know how good God was to the forefathers that today we all enjoy the land? Have they been told how obedience and disobedience to God can bring good or bad change in their lives? Maybe they have not been told about it, and this is why they don't believe.

It further explains why the freedom of religion mentioned in the First Amendment clause has lost purpose since we no longer practice our religions in general, we shall see why there is no more religion in us and what we can do about it in the following chapters.

We have lacked trust among ourselves, which has caused big divisions among us, not knowing and agreeing these divisions are not from God. We simply call it divergent views but it's more than what we have called it. The devil, through our selfishness and pride, is the root of all separations and divisions amongst us.

Too much can still be told about the forefathers, who passed the test of times and stayed faithful to God. How have we responded to this Word of God?

> Beware that you do not forget the LORD your God by not keeping His commandments, His judgments, and His statutes which I command you today, lest—when you have eaten and are full, and have built beautiful houses and dwell in them; and when your herds and your flocks multiply,

> and your silver and your gold are multiplied, and all that you have is multiplied; when your heart is lifted up, and you forget the LORD your God who brought you out of the land of Egypt, from the house of bondage.
>
> Deuteronomy 8:11-14 (NKJV)

This warning has failed us the people of God. Today all that the LORD promised and warned has happened in America, people have eaten and gotten full, have built beautiful houses and dwelt in them; and the herds and the flocks have also multiplied, Hasn't our silver and our gold multiplied America? Hasn't all that we've had multiplied, yet America has forgotten the LORD their God. "For the LORD your God is a consuming fire, a jealous God" (Deuteronomy 4:24, NKJV).

If we, the American people, can share in the blessing of God today for the obedience of our forefathers, why should we doubt if we can bring to ourselves judgment for our disobedience today? We overlook this truth about God. Life is what we make it, good or bad, by our obedience or disobedience to God.

> They have moved me to jealousy with that which is not God; they have provoked me to anger with their vanities: and I will move them to jealousy with those which are not a people; I will provoke them to anger with a foolish nation.
>
> Deuteronomy 32:21 (KJV)

God is love since he shows his love in many ways, just as we can individually mention. One of the things that proves the love of God is the life we have, the free air we breathe, and many uncountable things. We who can't decide our waking up, we could sleep and never wake up, yet we do wake up by the mercies of God. God gives life freely, yet he has put conditions to be fulfilled if we are to live in this life and land. He gave the same words to the forefathers by faith, because he said, "Be obedient so that you may prolong your days in the land which you shall possess." This means that for us to live in this possessed land, we must obey God to prolong our days.

For example, one can say he doesn't believe in anything, yet he believes in not believing in anything. He is so convinced into not believing in anything that he confesses that. The Bible says that out of the fullness of a man's heart he speaks. What people value they have kept into their hearts, and soon you will see their hearts through their speech, followed by actions that become habits, and then these repeated habits become their life.

What we say speaks big about what is in us. This is why Jesus told the ones that followed him,

> Either make the tree good and its fruit good, or else make the tree bad and its fruit bad; for a tree is known by its fruit. Brood of vipers! How can you, being evil, speak good things? For out of the abundance of the heart the mouth speaks. A good man out of the good treasure of his heart[g] brings forth good things, and an evil man out of the evil treasure brings forth evil things. But I say to you that for every idle word men may speak, they will give account of it in the Day of Judgment. For by your words you

> will be justified, and by your words you will be condemned."
>
> Matthew 12:33-37 (NKJV)

This portion of scripture explains the truth: that a person can't speak evil and be good. Although we can speak good and be evil, if a person's heart is full of anger, envy, bitterness, and greed, and the lusts of the world, it isn't surprising what they can speak; those words that have continually defiled America as a nation. For the forefathers spoke what filled their hearts, they desired to see a difference from where they had come from.

But what has happened to the present inhabitants that we have accepted to be corrupted in our hearts, believing in false doctrines .Just because this is what we call freedom.

God says:

> Although you know God, you have not glorified him as God. Nor are you thankful but have become futile in your thoughts and your foolish hearts have darkened. Professing to be wise, you have become fools and changed

the glory of the in corruptible God into an image made like corruptible man and birds and four footed beasts and creeping things. Therefore, God also has given you up to uncleanness in the lusts of your hearts to dishonour your bodies among yourselves. You exchanged the truth of God for the lie, and worshiped and served the creature rather than the creator who is blessed forever. Amen. For this reason, God has given you up to vile passions. For even your women exchange the natural use for what is against nature Likewise also the men leaving the natural use of the woman, burned in your lust for one another men with men committing what is shameful and receiving in themselves the penalty of your error which is due. And even as you did not like to retain God in your knowledge God gave you over to a debased mind to do those things which are not fitting. Being filled with all unrighteousness sexual immorality, wickedness, covetousness,

> maliciousness, full of envy, murder, strife, deceit, evilmindedness, you are whisperers, backbiters, haters of God, violent, proud, boasters, inventors of evil things, disobedient to parents, undiscerning, untrust-worthy, unloving, unforgiving, not merciful. You knowing the righteous judgement of God, that those who practice such things are worthy of death, not only do the same but also approve of those who practice them.
>
> Romans 1:21-32 (KJV)

Has what happened to the Romans then befallen the American people? Being that we fail to get time to examine our selves. The Roman Empire is no more, just as the devil crafts the American Empire to be no more. Discern these times.

To God, this is exactly what is happening in America. God has explained the cause, saying although we know God we have not glorified him as God in use of the religion freedom , clause nor are we thankful about the plenty that we have had over the years and the good life, but have instead become futile in our thoughts and our foolish hearts have been darkened.

This is what God calls the loss of freedom. This is when we call evil "good" and "normal," losing our conscience about what we definitely knew to be evil because we exercise our rights.

We are slaves to sin. Slavery to sin means we now live in the lusts of our heart, for we have exchanged the truth of God for a lie and worshiped and served the creature rather than the creator.

The creations in which we live have become more important to us than the creator of these creations. We have been taken up by what is perishing. May the Spirit of God help to reveal to us individually what these things are in our lives so that we will know what God is exactly talking about. You will need the holy spirit of God who comes into your life when you repent of your sins and live a life honouring and obedient to Jesus Christ as the Son of God, as LORD and saviour, living as he teaches we should live.

God is saying we who approve of evil practices are also worthy of death, and death meaning eternal hell when we don't repent and encourage others to repent. These practices and lawlessness as mentioned above in the scripture Romans 1:21-32 they are contrary to the will of God for us.

The Bible says:

> My people are destroyed from lack of knowledge. "Because you have rejected knowledge, I also reject you as my priests; because you have ignored the law of your God, I also will ignore your children."
>
> Hosea 4:6 (NKJV)

God refers to his knowledge as the truth in the Bible. When we ignore the law He has promised to ignore our children then this means the country will have no future since God will have ignored our children. America has been and will always be peaceful, free from wars and safe against attacks from other nations because of one special reason. God will protect us as he has always done if we will only give him the chance, by not trusting in power, money, technology, freedom—we can all testify that these are useless without the help of God.

Destruction can't be called upon; destructions come because of the devil. This is why Satan will do his work in us which is to steal, kill, and destroy. This is to shorten our days here and destroy our souls forever, but remember: this is contrary to what God has planned for us.

> For the eyes of the LORD range throughout the earth to strengthen those whose hearts are fully committed to him. You have done a foolish thing, and from now on you will be at war."
>
> 2 Chronicles 16:9 (NKJV)

Can this happen? We should pray for change in our lives; what opportunity have we given God to help us? We say we are powerful. Okay, God will watch from the side as we prove that power.

The choice to walk in all the ways of God, which he has commanded us, will keep and sustain us all the days of our life. This is the true freedom of America, only given by Jesus Christ, the son of the living God. For what we have today is a false freedom given by the devil. Look; fear is all around us.

THE PURPOSE OF GOD'S LEADING AMERICA

God can lead an individual, a group of people, an organization, and a nation if their decisions are made based on what is pure and proper in the sight of God. In these circumstances, God is the influence. These people will consult the Word of God for guidance and will work toward what pleases God. Thanks to God this is not a mystery anymore? We can learn about what pleases God from His Word, the Bible.

The God who knows all hearts will know our works toward pleasing Him; this is what we forget when we speak about ourselves before men, yet the one who qualifies our deeds sees our hearts and knows the motives of all that we do.

God's plan is to help the world come to the understanding that He is the creator and giver of life to all that have breath and to the dead. This has not been very smooth, as the Bible explains about the fall of man in Genesis. God doesn't give up on His plan of helping man to live a peaceful life on earth. For example, this is the very reason Jesus Christ came to be born here on earth so that He could live, die, and then be resurrected and live again as an assurance for the same that will choose to believe in him as their hope. God sent His son to work on bridging the gap between man and God, which leads man to receiving assistance from God Himself throughout the Holy Spirit. All things that God works out are to help man relate with Him, their creator. Just as we saw in the past chapters that God is the God for all, He is still open to become the LORD of all that believe in Him. God speaks through Jesus Christ about how simple and light His burden is when Jesus Christ calls all that are heavy burdened to come to Him and rest; these are very profound truths about life.

> At that time Jesus answered and said,
> "I thank You, Father, LORD of heaven

> and earth, that You have hidden these things from the wise and prudent and have revealed them to babes. Even so, Father, for so it seemed good in Your sight. All things have been delivered to me by My Father, and no one knows the Son except the Father. Nor does anyone know the Father except the Son, and the one to whom the Son wills to reveal Him. Come to Me, all you who labor and are heavy laden, and I will give you rest. Take My yoke upon you and learn from Me, for I am gentle and lowly in heart, and you will find rest for your souls. For My yoke is easy and My burden is light.
>
> Mathew 11: 25-30 (NKJV)

All that Jesus Christ said he does has been God's plan of leading and relating with man from the beginning. We learn this from the way He led the children of Israel and how He had planned greatness for them. For example, God's Word to the children of Israel through Moses was:

> Therefore be careful to observe them for this is your wisdom and your understanding in the sight of the people, who will hear all these statutes and say surely this great nation is a wise and understanding people.
>
> Deuteronomy 4:6 (KJV)

The Word of the LORD was told to the children of Israel, and it worked just as God had said it would work. We have heard and read about the greatness of David as king when all the children of Israel were known in the whole earth just as it this day. What about the wisdom of his son Solomon all written in the Bible?

What is not surprising is that the American people have been characterized by these words above over the years because God was leading.

For America is a great nation.

Americans are a wise people.

Americans are understanding people.

Surely look intently at yourselves, America followed the statutes and commandments of God, and, as God has declared, this has always been your wisdom and understanding in the sight of the people of the entire world. Like they said to Israel they have said this great nation is a wise and understanding people when referring to America.

God says that in the sight of other people the children of Israel were to be understanding and full of wisdom because of the laws and commandments. Hasn't this word happened for the American people? Haven't American people been understanding in the sight of the world? Isn't America a great nation?

During the times of the forefathers, God proved the above to be true to this day this all happened because God was leading. Testimonies of this truth are; Alexander Hamilton, a forefather, worked with the Rev James Bayard to form the Christian Constitutional Society, spreading across the world the two things which Hamilton said made America great: Christianity and a Constitution formed under Christianity.

"The Christian Constitutional Society's object was, and is first, the support of the Christian religion and the support of the United States.

"For my own part, I sincerely esteem it [the Constitution] a system which without the finger of God, never could have been suggested and agreed upon by such a diversity of interests," he said. [8]

In 1812, President Madison signed a federal bill which economically aided the Bible Society of Philadelphia in its goal of the mass distribution of the Bible.

"An Act for the relief of the Bible Society of Philadelphia." Approved February 2, 1813 by Congress.[9]

This is the only reason why America is what she is today. We have been lifted high among nations. It's easy to think we did something right so that America deserves the position of being most powerful and richest nation in the world. Yet things can prove us wrong if we thought like that. Without God, we can become anything other than powerful and great. The power is in Him whom our fathers worshiped and the plan He had to make us great. Have we noticed that He chose us, and if we can't appreciate this, then what will happen to us? We have witnessed all the good things our nation has done all around the world, yet today we are challenged by simple things like agreeing on something among ourselves. Our problems today are bigger than what we think, our enemy is cunning than we imagine and therefore solutions to our problems are not what we have concluded them to be. The problems are to be worked upon by all of us as a nation every person yielding to find answers from God.

Greatness has a source, and without this source such greatness is professed greatness which is short lived and so limited to accomplish anything significant. This is the kind of power and greatness anyone, any nation can get. We were separated and positioned this way by God. He believed in our forefathers' dreams and knew we would learn from them and keep their spirit for the land and God.

Not like what some are thinking, sighting change in the whole world, do we copy the world? They have always learned from us we have always had the answers through our relationship with God. Today we are in panic looking for answers from every where we can, never finding them because the answers are with God. He has never forsaken us; it is ourselves that have forsaken Him.

And, God continued to warn the children of Israel about the statutes and the good about observing them. "God spoke to the children of Israel, God said all the statutes are for you so that you may live" (Deuteronomy 4:1, KJV).

And these words were revealed to the forefathers, and they observed them with the help of the Holy Spirit, because of their faith in God. We know this because it happened, didn't it? Hasn't America lived in peace? For this very reason, America has not lived like any other country in the world, but has enjoyed stable peace for a long time which is challenged today.

Look at the good things like democracy, which is a good system of governance and how this has brought peace to the people that have practiced it, spreading through the whole world. Also, consider the many innovations in America and the many good researches for all the spheres of life; these have made America a channel of God's blessing to the world.

Look at all the aid given out to other countries to save lives. From what God has multiplied we have massively spent to make the world a convenient place in times of need. Isn't this a sign of an understanding people just as the scripture has mentioned above. God sees all that and thanks us for that heart, although this giving cannot replace obedience to God. Remember, obedience is better than sacrifice.

But Samuel replied:

> "Does the Lord delight in burnt offerings and sacrifices as much as in obeying the Lord?
> To obey is better than sacrifice,
> and to heed is better than the fat of rams. For rebellion is like the sin of divination, and arrogance like the evil of idolatry. Because you have rejected the word of the Lord,
> he has rejected you as king," God said to Saul through Samuel.
>
> 1 Samuel 15:22 (NKJV)

Obedience is better than sacrifice, and in our case we are to accept the Lord to lead us and be obedient; in other words, we shall continue to be a blessing to other nations, not because we have, but because we shall see need being that the Lord will be leading. What we have in the land we shall be willing to share out of obedience, and if our eyes can't see what we have already, how shall we give?

Of course, someone will say; when we don't have, then others have, but are they going to share with the rest, or will they share with us since we may not have anymore? To many, sharing might be so hard for them. We need systems in place that enables the dollar to go from its source but come back so that the cycle is complete that was the plan. It can't only go without the means of returning. What this will turn into is lack. The devil's plan and concern is that since we have chosen to be disobedient to God, why should we enjoy the fruits of obedience. So the knowledge to enable the dollar to come back should be scarce among us which will lead us to lack and test the cost of disobedience in this case.

The devil planned that we become reluctant to do a check on what goes out and how it would return through the proper channels. This turns the country into dependents, not on God as of old, but dependent on man.

A bagger is vulnerable; he is used; he says yes to anything because of lack. This is the devil's plan if we are to stay glued to his ideas of becoming the ones in need like the rest of the world. He has planned to take away all that has been accomplished for many years, he will fail if we heed to the voice of God.

We are losing the control of this particular blessing, although blessings encompass several things. This particular blessing is shifting from us to another people, who are most likely going to misuse the dollar for something other than glorifying God as we had done for a long time.

And since we have seen and known the truth, this truth of what makes the country great should be told to all who plan to join this "land of plenty." This is the truth for the good of the land and for their own good.

Telling them that this land has gone through much trouble and He God is the only one that helped. Its plenty is dependent on the obedience to God, not the hardworking of the inhabitants or its currency, the dollar, because although people are hard working and want to work, they can still be unemployed; although the source of the dollar is right here in America the country can sadly still borrow.

This doesn't mean forcing them into believing, but this helps them to understand that we behave the way we behave because we chose to do so for God. it's because if they are not told the source of why they are choosing to come, when they have come, they will become leaders who will unknowingly think they are bringing change from elsewhere, which ends up to being misleading.

We should be loving; we should explain to them that such ideas make it very hard for God to lead us and have caused failure to the ones that practice them.

America is not just that land of immigrants, but it's a land of immigrants who have a purpose—to serve God through Jesus Christ's example freely. This is the only reason, and it's not what many have changed the reason to be as we have seen in the previous chapters. And if we inhabitants, the American people, can't attach value to what has been given to us freely, how can we protect it?

This is true with the lawlessness and neglect of the commandments of God, which has increased in America today. Sin is compromised among us. What God is saying to all Americans is that we must first acknowledge the source of the greatness of our country. This helps us to do all that it takes to protect this greatness, which is a result of obeying God, and it should be done regardless of origin, color, or race, just in oneness of purpose and united.

Watch, if God is not given chance to lead through the circumstances that allow Him to lead, then Satan leads us and is leading America. The devil inspires our decisions as a nation insofar as we have even unknowingly given him access to our finances, where we have sponsored and supported issues that are openly, without doubt, against the will of God for man.

Remember, when we distance ourselves from God, the devil swiftly comes into our lives, uninvited, of course, for where there is no light, darkness occupies, and vice versa is true.

The consequences of our present disobedience will cause our greatness to be exchanged for weakness, our being wise to becoming foolish.

This will be the opposite of what God intended. He trusted us and made us custodians of law to spread it throughout the world so He gave us wealth (power of the dollar) for this reason that we all share with the rest of the world.

No one will help if we stop helping being that need is going to rise all around.

God will be around to help and, should He choose others to help just because we disobeyed, we must be willing to repent instead. Only listen to what the spirit tells the nation: we shall see the salvation of the LORD.

But closing our eyes from seeing and acknowledging something is going wrong doesn't exempt us from the torment of the devil.

It can look and seem like we are not concerned for any reason yet we see others hurting. God is warning that "let not these days change us, because these are the last days with the exact signs given by Jesus Christ" (Mathew 24:3-31). As many turn away from the truth, we need to remain who we have always been: a wise and understanding people, and a great nation.

For example, several years ago it was so safe to live in America. Today, it seems so worrying to live in America. Evil has surrounded us from all directions. People are free to do all sorts of evil all in the name of rights. This kind of living seems okay today, but will cause calamities for the American people, and will cost the nation greatly.

As we have continued to only speak about God and have failed to honor him in our actions. Today we say we know God, but have no respect of God evident in how we treat ourselves and our neighbors. Such living is not worthy of a nation in our capacity; a country loved and protected by faith, a country founded on the promises of God.

We, the American people, have become our own enemies. We have become enemies to the truth, practicing the truth in partiality, doing only those things that are convenient, and not obeying God. Remember, the Word of God warns,

> And be not conformed to this world: but be ye transformed by the renewing of your mind, that ye may prove what is that good, and acceptable, and perfect, will of God.
>
> Romans 12:2 (KJV)

Jesus asked this question

For what shall it profit a man, if he shall gain the whole world, and lose his own soul? Or what shall a man give in exchange for his soul? Whosoever therefore shall be ashamed of me and of my words in this adulterous and sinful generation; of him also shall the Son of man be ashamed, when he cometh in the glory of his Father with the holy angels (Mark 8:36-38, KJV).

Today, the teaching of Jesus Christ doesn't have room in our hearts. We are ashamed of the name of Jesus Christ and ashamed of being religious. When we talk about how we pray to God in secret, we end our conversations by denying being religious people. Why should we be ashamed of being religious? This fear among us to shy away from being religious is a complete denial of the LORD before many, perhaps because we are afraid of being judged by the people around us. We should be happy when they judge us it's for our good to stay in the faith because of their judgments. We are religious let us be willing to live as our talk, this is the only way to a righteous life. We shy away from Jesus yet the forefathers believed Jesus Christ and his teaching. This brought such tremendous favor from God.

God knew we were going to act as our forefathers, but have instead devoted more resources and time working out ways of being different from them, for the sake of it. These have been and are the devil's traps.

Surprisingly because of our position and prosperity other people will look at how we live and want to be just like us saying if they the great live like that what problem is it if we live just like them. You notice that being blessed with all that we have and have heard was for a purpose and that the world would know God and the LORD Jesus

Christ. But the devil wants to prove that we are not the best to be trusted for this purpose. God's plan is not going to change. We are to teach and be examples to all nations on how to love, care, and worship God, in truth and in spirit. God wants this to be done as He purposed for the land.

Instead, the devil has claimed the land and the souls in it, saying, how should they claim to be Christians or the people of God if they can't live as people of God. He is making us teach the world how to sin against God, using the position, the power, and the money God has given to us. This is so that he (the devil) can spread his plans of destroying the world through us. Shame, and a big shame on the devil. His plan failed, the LORD exposed him, and He will continue to expose him always.

God still loves America, just as He loves and cares for the whole world. He has plans of taking all of us, the whole world, with Him to heaven. This is for all who will believe in the only son of God, Jesus Christ, because He is the way, the truth, and the life. How shall we know the way except He shows it to us, this encompasses many things.

While God was leading, several good unspeakable things have been happening. God has risen up several spirit-filled teachers, presidents, judges, managers, preaches, apostles, evangelists, intercessors, fathers, mothers, sons, and daughters, spirit-filled meaning "a reflection of being inspired by and used divinely of God." In all the different churches, governments, businesses, schools people who have been given to serving God, people given to prayer and the truth of God's Word. This is evident when we send missionaries all around the world, seen in the efforts to spread the Word of God with the many men of God who are serving, teaching God's Word in America and over the world.

This has its root from the understanding that the Word of God transforms life. This has been done right from the times of Thomas Jefferson because he said, "The doctrines of Jesus are simple, and tend to all the happiness of man. Of all the systems of morality, ancient or modern, which have come under my observation, none appears to me so pure as that of Jesus." [10]

Could you have any doubt about what Jesus Christ does and how much he can change someone individually? By taking Jesus Christ's teaching away from public schools and from the public is a declaration of saying, "Satan, come and reign in our country." Remember, Satan's purpose never changes. He is in the world to steal, kill, and destroy. He might approach gently and give ideas that do not seem harmful, but he has a purpose to destroy America, and through America, to destroy the whole world. We shall see this and how he had planned it as we study and read through the chapters ahead.

But concerning about the Word of God in the times of Moses .God said through Moses,

"You shall not add to the word which I command you, nor take from it, that you may keep the commandments of the LORD your God which I command you" (Deuteronomy 4:2 KJV).

As God warned he is warning today because people around the world are changing God's Word to suit their desires as we live in these last days. There is no fear of God. People have forgotten that he is a forgiving and a holy God, which implies he will forgive anyone who accepts their wrong but sadly punish anyone for not accepting his forgiveness.

> For God so loved the world that He gave His only begotten Son, that whoever believes in Him should not

> perish but have everlasting life. For God did not send His Son into the world to condemn the world, but that the world through Him might be saved.
>
> "He who believes in Him is not condemned; but he who does not believe is condemned already, because he has not believed in the name of the only begotten Son of God.
>
> John 3:16-18 (NKJV)

Accepting the forgiveness of God is repenting which is acknowledging that one is wrong because all have sinned and have fallen short of the glory of God (Romans 3:23, NKJV), but more to that repentance is a change from doing what was pleasing in our hearts to what God says is right, many times what we have known to be good is not necessary what God approves as right before Him. We do what we know without care of what God says about it. For example we have known that it's okay to be angry because we were wronged by someone. It sounds so natural in that this person or people wronged us so we must fill how we fill.

What is truth is that Jesus says forgive that your sins can be forgiven, If we can't forgive our brother for a wrong then our sins cannot be forgiven by our father in heaven.

"And whenever you stand praying, if you have anything against anyone, forgive him, that your Father in heaven may also forgive you your trespasses. But if you do not forgive, neither will your Father in heaven forgive your trespasses" (Mark 11: 25-26).

More about anger is studied in (Ephesians 4:26-27, NKJV): "Be angry, and do not sin: do not let the sun go down on your wrath, nor give place to the devil."

People who love and serve God can't accommodate sin in their lives, because such people know what the Bible says: "For it is written, 'Be holy, for I am holy,' says the LORD" (1 Peter 1:16, KJV).

God loves sinners if they are forsaking sin to repent, meaning they are turning from sin to obedience. Compromising with sin, claiming he created us in that sinful way, or even denying sin because people have decided to define what sin is in their own terms without using what the book (Bible) shows them to be sin. This is all being blind. This is the misconception about God in America, and it is making sin look acceptable today. Blame is put on society yet we are the society ourselves.

As you read, acknowledge the sin in your life today and decide to change. God loves sinners, and so he changes them from sinners into righteous sons through the LORD Jesus. But we must be able to acknowledge sin and so accept forgiveness from Jesus Christ as our forefathers once did.

John Hancock said,

> In circumstances as dark as these, it becomes us, as Men and Christians, to reflect that whilst every prudent measure should be taken to ward off the impending judgments,...at the same time all confidence must be withheld from the means we use; and reposed only on that God rules in the armies of Heaven, and without His whole blessing, the best human counsels are but foolishness....
>
> Resolved...Thursday the eleventh of May...to humble themselves before God under the heavy judgments felt and feared, to confess

> the sins that have deserved them, to implore the Forgiveness of all our transgressions, and a spirit of repentance and reformation…and a Blessing on the…Union of the American Colonies in Defence of their Rights [for which hitherto we desire to thank Almighty God].[xi]

A day of fasting was declared in America. This can still happen today don't we need forgiveness about the many things that have interrupted our relationship with God. "What great nation is there that has God so near to it as the LORD our God is to us, for whatever reason we may call upon him?" (Deuteronomy 4:7, KJV).

> These are the words to the children of Israel during their early days. Since we now know how God works through his word let us depend on this word to perfectly work for us. We have different reasons. The Bible says whatever reason that we can call upon him let us call upon him. Let us call

upon him for help to a walk that is pleasing to Him. Let us call on him for guidance about the decisions we make as a nation. Let us call on him to forgive our sins. Let us call on him for direction as a nation. Call on in the white house. Let us call on him in the Congress and senate for guidance. Let us call on him for guidance on how the Bible should be taught in school. Let us call on him in times of any need individually. Call on him as a family, Call on him as a church, as a community, and as a nation. Let us call on him. This is how close we should be to God. He is waiting for our call on him in repentance. We are encouraged by His Word.

If my people who are called by my name will handle themselves and pray and seek my face and turn from their wicked ways, then I will hear from heaven and will forgive their sin and heal their land, for this is the greatest urgent need of the American people.

2 Chronicles 7:14 (KJV)

THE STATE OF AMERICA'S FAMILY

America's family life has been challenged by several pressures, to the extent that we have given up on all the benefits that come by having true family as seen by the plan of God. To fully overcome some of these challenges surrounding family, we must find the truth about family in God's Word. God gave several words of encouragement to the children of Israel that would help them live in godly families, explaining the importance of it.

God began family in the very beginning, just like he instituted marriage when he created a man and a woman. Both man and woman were given the primary duty of looking after each other for Eve was a companion of Adam.

"Therefore, a man shall leave his father and mother and be joined to his wife, and they shall become one flesh. And they were both naked, the man and his wife, and were not ashamed" (Genesis 2: 24-25, NKJV).

This was before Adam and Eva sinned against God. God had already planned about their being joined man and woman to become husband and wife who were to bear children as a way of multiplying. The Bible explains,

> So God created man in His own image; in the image of God He created him; male and female He created them. Then God blessed them, and God said to them, "Be fruitful and multiply; fill the earth and subdue it; have dominion over the fish of the sea, over the birds of the air, and over every living thing that moves on the earth."
>
> Genesis 1:27-28 (NKJV)

Adam and Eve where to stay with each other, help each other in love, and raise their children together growing in joy. From the times of Adam and Eve, this was to continue to be for every man and woman, so God gave ways in which family would continue with his knowledge in their midst so that man would enjoy his time on the earth.

It pleases God when we live in joy. So God warned the children of Israel.

> Only take heed to yourselves and diligently keep yourself, lest you forget the things your eyes have seen, and lest they depart from your heart all the days of your life. And teach them to your children and your grandchildren.
>
> Deuteronomy 4:9 (NKJV)

God was warning the children of Israel to be careful, saying that; "one day, when you have crossed to the promised land, after a long time has passed, be careful to diligently keep yourself, lest you forget the things your eyes have seen and lest they depart from your heart all the days of your life. For this is how future generations will learn why you live and behave the way you behave, by teaching your children and Grandchildren this same law and its benefits.

God was showing them how they were to preserve the law in their land, and this was to be the only way the land was to remain sanctified. God told the children of Israel to teach their children his commandments, because these events were a basis for their survival. Without them, their nation wouldn't have existed. To them, this was the reason for their existence: loving God and obeying God showing the same practices to their Children primarily in a family setting. God continues to warn them,

> Hear, O Israel: The LORD our God, the LORD is one! You shall love the LORD your God with all your heart, with all your soul, and with all your strength. And these words which I command you today shall be in your heart. You shall teach them diligently to your children, and shall talk of them when you sit in your house, when you walk by the way, when you lie down, and when you rise up. You

> shall bind them as a sign on your hand, and they shall be as frontlets between your eyes. You shall write them on the doorposts of your house and on your gates.
>
> Deuteronomy 6:4-9 (NKJV)

God put emphasis to all the times the children where with their parents these where times to study the law of God for example, he says; "you shall teach them diligently to your children, and shall talk of them when you sit in your house, when you walk by the way, when you lie down, and when you rise up. He speaks about Parents teaching their children because He knows the parents met together to study the law.

Do we read our Bibles in our homes as a family so that the children can learn from us? This responsibility was given to the fathers and mothers first and should be considered carefully.

God is giving this responsibility to the parents. Note that God says what we teach shall come from our hearts. This means parents must become the first disciples of Christ, and so will show and teach their children what should be done.

This further meant that Israel's tomorrow was dependent on the Israel of that time as America's tomorrow is dependent on today's fathers and mothers and how they raise their children. The future is done today through the children, they are the presidents, judges, teachers and mums and fathers of tomorrow. It's we who have the future of America in our hands, especially with the way we shall raise up our children. If our children see us, the dad just mistreating their mum, or see their mum mistreating their dad, this is who they will become; because we have already denied them the knowledge to know God by the way we carry ourselves. We can also misrepresent God in the way we behave, we must be mindful of this too.

Children are the fruits of the womb, a blessing to the father and mother, because children will one day grow up to look after their parents. They must be loved and cared for equally. A good life for our kids will only spring from the love and our fear of God. God will help us love our family if we decide to fear God. Raising children is our responsibility that shouldn't worry us as parents if we do the right thing. Children shouldn't just grow to live and be what they want to be, because some may want to be bad because of bad influence. It's a child's right to choose who she or he wants to be, yet it's a parent's responsibility to raise him or her in the fear of God. God warns us, "And, ye fathers provoke not our children to wrath: but bring them up in the nurture and admonition of the LORD" (Ephesians 6:4 KJV).

Do we see ourselves showing our children the law and commandments of God? Please, do our children see us living a life obedient to God? Or for example, we have taught them to say lies: "Tell him that I am not at home yet we are at home." What we are now is what our children will become; because we are at times their source of values. If we are greedy, corrupt, filled with wrath and hatred, then this is exactly what our children will become. We can avoid this by changing our lives. This is the time to save our families.

What is important is the mindset of how we view ourselves and our responsibilities when we decide to get married, man to woman. Today marriage has changed its purpose and meaning to us. It's "what do I get from this marriage when it doesn't work out?" We think about how it might fail to work out more than what we must do to let it work out. We end up worrying all the time about our marriage with this in mind: "one day it might fail to work out". Such a mindset gives small room to developing a relationship with our spouse; in fact, it makes no way for the things that can be of benefit to the children. We fight about who will be more liked by the children in case things don't work out. We have led our children to having a preference between mum and dad. They should be able to love and respect both of us without preference; kids belong to both of us. Remember, God said two shall be one body. It could be that the two may have had different plans in the beginning, and then through agreement, God who let us meet will help us find a common ground which will begin with our values in the LORD.

This will make homes be what God intended them to be, full of love, with no violence.

> Between us as spouses we should work towards a faithful marriage with love, this is what love is; Love suffers long and is kind; love does not envy; love does not parade itself, is not puffed up; does not behave rudely, does not seek its own, is not

> provoked, thinks no evil; does not rejoice in iniquity, but rejoices in the truth; bears all things, believes all things, hopes all things, endures all things.
>
> Love never fails...
>
> (1 Corinthians 13:4–8 NKJV)

We should stay a family, with mums and dads, for a child to develop character and grow into an aspiring father or mother, with love for his or her family and children.

Freedom has been abused so that children in America decide their ways; they are not to be counseled by even their own mums and dads. What parent would have a child and wish failure for them? Parents have always loved their children, and advised them about making good choices and wise decisions. The children have instead quoted their rights, in the process leaving their parents with folded hands. Do parents have good ideas worth listening to? Yes, they do. Yet America's freedom has made them speechless; many or all of us have lost our freedom when it comes to our own kids. Kids have caused tremendous pain by how they live in their disobedience; is that freedom for us as the parents?

Who would want their children to suffer? Or who would want their children to become disobedient children? Yet too much freedom without the stand of saying no to them (kids) about the many things they are involved in will in the end bring the opposite of what we want them to become.

God's Word says to our children,

> Children, obey your parents in the LORD: for this is right.
>
> Honor thy father and mother; (which is the first commandment with promise) that it may be well with thee and you may live long on the earth.
>
> Ephesians 6:1-3 (KJV)

Children are told to obey their parents as a command from God in the LORD, for this is right. It's God's advice through his Word. What we discover is that children are using their rights to disobey not only the parents, but unknowingly disobey the Word of God, as Ephesians 6:1 above has said. As they disobey, unknowingly, they are missing out on the promise in verse 3, which says; that it may be well with you and that you may live long on the earth.

The American children have no future if we take note of the scripture as from God's Word, because they (children) are not obeying their parents. Do we now see why the Bible is very important, this was noticed by the forefathers and in the coming chapters we shall look at what their plan was when responding to this importance, they knew that in the Bible as mentioned earlier springs; the issues of life.

What options have we given God? What can He do more if His word already gives solutions but we have disregarded it? We think we are putting God out of our business so that our lives will be free, but this continues to make us slaves of the devil, who wants us to disobey God and be destroyed with him in his punishment in hell.

This is God's concern. He created us and loves us more than we love ourselves. Yet He is limited to His Word. We push ourselves away from near Him, how is He going to help? Who loses when we walk in our own ways? Apart from God, who sent his only begotten son to suffer and die so that we become free from the punishment of sin, apart from Jesus who knows that the torment in hell is such a pain that no one of us deserves to face. Who else cares?

He is God. He is not going to change to be like us. If we need life, we are to change to do what he says is right for us, not what we think is good for us.

How will our children know all the above and more of God unless they are taught. Children are so neglected that there is such a big gap within families. Remember, they are sent to daycare centers, schools, and most of the time the children are not with their dad or mum, spending most of their early years in school. With the tight schedule of trying to make ends meet coupled with a stressful atmosphere, we can even fail to attend church with them. How will our kids ever know about Jesus Christ and the love of God for them and all of us if they are not helped? What about the importance of obeying parents?

We should not expect much from them if we are not giving them the choice. They watch what we do; they copy and do, they hear what we say so they say it also. We can avoid this. God wonders how forgetful the American people have become. Do we consider the truth that America's tomorrow is entirely determined by the children of America today?

In America today, marriage is seen as a troubling issue among the many troubles of life; this is affecting the children who have just faced a rough time from their parents. They don't deserve any of our hardheartedness; they are innocent.

The failure to forgive each other has caused the divorce rate to go high. The devil plans to create such uncertainty about marriage that the next generations will be afraid of marriage. Saying, "Why should we be married? After all, it never works out."

People get into marriage for fun to the extent that we now sign a contract to stay just months or years with our spouse. Such habits sound like freedom, but the one who inspires and causes them is so committed to destroying this nation by using ourselves, the American people. If we say we shouldn't care, we are exercising our rights, but who would care to love us and this nation and to protect us from the devil, who is making us enemies of God unless we begin to care.

What will the world say about us the people of God? What will the people say about our God then? Please, if you plan to divorce for any reason, remember that this could destroy your life and the life of your children. Carefully evaluate your decision to divorce. What are your plans? What are your dreams? Why should you not reconcile; marriage is one of the most sought achievements of life. Marriage is what we make it ourselves and by understanding this, what makes you think it will be better if you had another spouse since it might be yourself that fails your present marriage. Marriage is so precious to God that He created man and woman for this very reason that they would enjoy the earth together. What you are about to do by divorcing is trampling under your feet the most valuable gift to man and woman. It's your right, but both of you might never, ever get your lives back. Think twice.

The exact idea behind this feeling we sometimes have about separating, is so that we mess up our lives and our children's life, then the devil will be happy that we chose his idea. The devil is a loser. We are not like him, for we are winners through Jesus Christ who will do anything to save us from the devil's traps. What life is the devil planning to give us here on earth that must cost us the opportunity to live with God for ever in heaven? Sorry for some of us who have had these bad experiences already, God through Jesus Christ his son can give us a new beginning if we decide to have our lives back. Give your heart to the LORD Jesus to fix your heart if it was broken. When we give our hearts to Jesus no relationship will break our hearts, we might get some pain but we can never be broken because even when our hearts are broken our God will mend them through his love and care.

Jesus teaches about divorce and marriage, in a way that has been avoided today, avoiding it doesn't change the truth about it. It remains as he taught it because he wants us to learn something. This is when the Pharisees asked him about the same issue.

> And the Pharisees came to him, and asked him, "Is it lawful for a man to put away his wife?" Tempting him.
>
> And he answered and said unto them, what did Moses command you?
>
> And they said, Moses suffered to write a bill of divorcement, and to put her away.

> And Jesus answered and said unto them, for the hardness of your heart he wrote you this precept.
>
> But from the beginning of the creation God made them male and female.
>
> For this cause shall a man leave his father and mother, and cleave to his wife;
>
> And they twain shall be one flesh: so then they are no more twain, but one flesh.
>
> What therefore God hath joined together, let not man put asunder.
>
> And in the house his disciples asked him again of the same matter.
>
> And he saith unto them, whosoever shall put away his wife, and marries another commits adultery against her.
>
> And if a woman shall put away her husband, and be married to another, she committeth adultery.
>
> Mark 10:2-12 (NKJV)

Jesus is teaching us to be contented with whoever is our spouse and love them; otherwise divorce is a complete sin before God. Apart from divorce being sin it will be hard for a mum or a dad alone to bring up an innocent child in the fear of God. Remember, he has nothing to do with both of us not forgiving each other, dad and mum. Where do we get the idea of not saying sorry to our spouse? What if we were wrong about the divorce? Can't we go to him or her to ask for forgiveness? Put away shame and pride you can go back and ask for forgiveness.

All has gone wrong in America; we are even finding it hard to define marriage, looking for definitions that will fit our desires. God's Word is the standard, and it's a waste of time and resources to imagine God will change to be like man, He is God, and it's us men and women who must change and be obedient to God through his Word, the Bible and it's for our own good.

This is what he wants life to be, the Bible declares:

> So God created man in his [own] image, in the image of God created he him; male and female created he them.
>
> And God blessed them, and God said unto them, be fruitful, and

> multiply, and replenish the earth, and subdue it: and have dominion over the fish of the sea, and over the fowl of the air, and over every living thing that moves upon the earth.
>
> Genesis 1:27-28 (KJV)

This is the plan of God: for man to multiply and subdue the earth. Today we must have noticed what numbers mean when it comes to anything; population counts, too. Why should we restrict our lives to one kid?

If for example, two families each have one son or one daughter and these two daughters or these two sons from these two families decide to have a same-sex marriage as it has been encouraged today, they will not be able to bear children. How will these two families ever multiply?

This kind of life evidently disobeys God's command of multiplication, as we have read in the scripture above. God destroyed Sodom and Gomorrah just for this very abomination among other practices, The Bible says, "Then the LORD rained upon Sodom and upon Gomorrah brimstone and fire from the LORD out of heaven" (Genesis 19:24, KJV).

As mentioned in the Scriptures, that same-sex couple as a relationship results from someone being trapped by the devil, just like another can be trapped into lies or pride. Today, for example, a liar, a thief, or a prostitute will repent of their sins, but someone who practices these acts of same sex will never repent, because he or she has been made to believe that he or she was created like this.

We have told them a lie in efforts of gaining popularity, cheap perishing gains, yet we don't discover that when we do that we have become hypocrites before God. We know the truth, but have kept silent to prove to the world how good and blameless we are.

Why not give them a chance to speak out so that we can know how to help them?

Please note that homosexuals are not bad people like some can imagine, and please don't think that anyone who tells them the truth is being impolite. They must be loved like anybody else, yet they ought to know the truth about their practice so that they will make informed decisions about it.

What shall we gain if we let them to believe they have no choice? We will only bring a curse upon our lives and their lives for collaborating with the devil, in the name of sympathy, yet destroying these dear ones.

Please, God loves them and doesn't want any one of them to perish in their sins. They have a choice of turning away from this trap if they repent and come to Jesus Christ.

We have not taken the trouble to find out about their lives so that we can pray to God with them for their freedom. Many have had relationships that didn't work out; some do this to earn a living. Some think this is their only way out. Whatever reason they have for these practices, we have not helped them in love and have not cared for them, yet we know the righteous judgment of God.

"That those who practice such things are worthy of death, not only do the same but also approve of those who practice them" (Romans 1:21-32, KJV).

We have encouraged them because we have looked for perishing gains from them.

The truth is that such acts are sins just like all sin against God. However just like any other sins and disobediences there is a punishment. For the devil who tempts us to sin against God has planned to take all of us with him to hell as he himself has been judged. Already he waits to serve his eternal punishment in hell's fire he roars like a lion.

God warns us, "Be sober, be vigilant; because your adversary the devil walks about like a roaring lion, seeking whom he may devour. Resist him, steadfast in the faith, knowing that the same sufferings are experienced by your brotherhood in the world" (1 Peter 5:8-9, NKJV).

He is seeking whom he may devour, because he is already judged for his sins and his angels as Jesus Christ helps us to understand this in Matthew.

Then He will also say to those on the left hand, "Depart from Me, you cursed, into the everlasting fire prepared for the devil and his angels: for I was hungry and you gave Me no food; I was thirsty and you gave Me no drink; I was a stranger and you did not take Me in, naked and you did not clothe Me, sick and in prison and you did not visit Me." (Mathew 25:41-43, NKJV)

This is what God teaches about sin and temptation in James:

> Blessed is the man who endures temptation; for when he has been approved, he will receive the crown of life which the LORD has promised to those who love Him. Let no one say when he is tempted, "I am tempted by God"; for God cannot be tempted by evil, nor does He Himself tempt anyone. But each one is tempted when he is drawn away by his own desires and enticed. Then, when desire has conceived, it gives birth to sin; and sin, when it is full-grown, brings forth death.
>
> Do not be deceived, my beloved brethren. Every good gift and every perfect gift is from above, and comes down from the Father of lights, with whom there is no variation or shadow of turning.
>
> James 1:12-17 (NKJV)

This is why Jesus Christ paid a price when he died on the cross for every one's sins, that whoever will believe in him will not perish, but will have eternal life (John 3:16). Jesus also came to give us the power to resist sin in our lives when temptations show up in our minds. He wants us to be pure and righteous.

> And you know that He was manifested to take away our sins, and in Him there is no sin. Whoever abides in Him does not sin. Whoever sins has neither seen Him nor known Him.
>
> Little children, let no one deceive you. He who practices righteousness is righteous, just as He is righteous. He who sins is of the devil, for the devil has sinned from the beginning. For this purpose the Son of God was manifested, that He might destroy the works of the devil. Whoever has been born of God does not sin, for His seed remains in him; and he cannot sin, because he has been born of God.
>
> The Imperative of Love
>
> In this the children of God and the children of the devil are manifest: Whoever does not practice righteousness is not of God, nor is he who does not love his brother. For this is the message that you heard

> from the beginning, that we should
> love one another.
>
> 1 John 3:5-11 (NKJV)

Sin has consequences but our work is that we must love as God loves them, moreover we must tell the truth in love as the Scriptures have testified.

What God expected from us, the American people, the people of God, is that we ought to have wisely dealt with this issue. Knowing the righteous judgment of God, we should try everything possible in love to help these dear ones from these dangerous practices.

Not in hating them, but with love, clearly showing them that they wouldn't have existed if their parents had chosen to live this way of same-sex marriage. Also, showing them from the Bible how this is one of the sins among the many sins inspired by the devil.

The Bible mentions the cause for these and other practices in Roman 1:21-32.

Don't point fingers at them, but pray with them as they come out to speak about this practice. Churches, synagogues, temples can even help by developing centers for research in communities about these practices. With this becoming a way of life, then all the plans of God has been put on hold; meanwhile, the devil is busy convincing many through ourselves the parents and teachers in schools. How will family and all its benefits ever exist if the people choose to neglect its benefits?

And for the issues pertaining marriage, it should not be over as we have ruled it. God is willing to help in all ways so let us start praying and discussing the importance of family in society and all the blessing of God which are to begin in His only described definition of family.

God is ready to help.

THE STATE OF AMERICA'S EDUCATION SYSTEM

Education in America has been very successful for such a long time. Innovations and research have been the norm in the country. What we shall find out is how this was possible, because to this day we all still wonder how someone looks at nature to create the artificial things, like the bulb, a flying plane, the computer; what power is behind such mind? Was it in schools? If it was in school, in what kind of setting?

Like the previous chapters, our findings have been from the Bible, because it has all the answers to all questions. In the previous chapter we looked at the need of family and the benefits of family as it was according to God. One of the most distinctive benefits was that from childhood, children where to be taught about God's law which today is symbolic to the Bible.

We begin with the Bible among all books and teachings, because the fear of God is the beginning of all wisdom. "The fear of the LORD is the beginning of wisdom, and the knowledge of the Holy One is understanding" (Proverbs 9:10, NKJV).

The fear of God should come first and then knowledge can follow for knowledge to profit. No wonder this is why God told the children of Israel to teach their children about Himself (God). In obedience to the Word of God the forefathers understood what this meant.

James Madison, once wrote that,

> We've staked our future on our ability to follow the Ten Commandments with all of our heart.
>
> We have staked the whole future of American civilization, not upon the power of government, far from it. We've staked the future of all our political institutions upon our capacity...to sustain ourselves according to the Ten Commandments of God.[11]

Where are we staking our future today? Is it still in the Ten Commandments as the forefathers believed, or is it somewhere else?

So Noah Webster said:

> The duties of men are summarily comprised in the Ten Commandments, consisting of two tables; one comprehending the duties which we owe immediately to God-the other, the duties we owe to our fellow men.
>
> In my view, the Christian religion is the most important and one of the first things in which all children, under a free government ought to be instructed…No truth is more evident to my mind than that the Christian religion must be the basis of any government intended to secure the rights and privileges of a free people.[12]

To the forefathers, the Word of God was so important. This is why they developed a simpler way of working towards this responsibility of teaching their children the law, which is the Bible. They knew this was a primary responsibility, so God gave them knowledge and the ways, using schools for this responsibility. Schools were used as an additional avenue, because children spend most of their early days in school. What was taught in schools mattered so much because the future is shaped by what the children will practice when their time comes to become the leaders, presidents, Judges, teachers. The forefathers couldn't neglect the opportunity to use schools as determinant of America's tomorrow. The leaders especially presidents took it upon them selves to encourage the inhabitants and government to be part of the responsibility by helping the process of learning the Bible. This is the type of leadership that lasts, in that when they are gone we still remember their braveness and inspiring Words honoring God.

After all, God is all in all. Who among the doctors today could become a doctor without him having life, or who could be a scientist without studying nature which we know is all created by the God of the Bible. In other words, there is no science without God or nature. So as children studied nature, they studied who created nature, which is in God's Word; no wonder the big success in science (innovations). What is on their curriculums today, do we care to find out? We have neglected what is taught to the children, what are the motives of the curriculum?

In Benjamin Franklin's 1749 plan of education for public schools in Pennsylvania, he insisted that schools teach "the Excellency of the Christian religion above all others, ancient or modern."

In 1787, when Franklin helped found Benjamin Franklin University, it was dedicated as "a nursery of religion and learning, built on Christ, the Cornerstone."

Continuing, Benjamin Rush said,

> If moral precepts alone could have reformed mankind, the mission of the Son of God into our world would have been unnecessary.
>
> Let the children who are sent to those schools be taught to read and write and above all, let both sexes be carefully instructed in the principles and obligations of the Christian

> religion. This is the most essential part of education.[13]

The forefathers knew that their children and the grandchildren of America would need to know what brought success to them as forefathers.

Putting God first above all things, in acknowledging that the success of the country was dependent on God, they worked toward teaching all children the word of God in schools.

> Let divines and philosophers, statesmen and patriots, unite their endeavors to renovate the age by impressing the minds of men with the importance of educating their little boys and girls, inculcating in the minds of youth the fear and love of the Deity…and leading them in the study and practice of the exalted virtues of the Christian system.

They knew schools were a great avenue to reach out to children, so that all are given the opportunity to learn the Word of God. This idea was such a success, but the devil came in and disrupted this whole setting just like that.

It was through the misuse of freedom in America that led to that situation, because it is through freedom that our children aren't taught the very source of this freedom. Freedom has instead done harm in that it has blinded dads and mums from their only one responsibility: which is teaching their children in the ways of God. By missing this one, we have missed every good for their future. The children will face every kind of evil that awaits them; the dear ones won't even know to whom to run to for help.

God tells us through the Bible, "Train up a child in the way he should go, and when he is old he will not depart from it" (Proverbs 22:6, NKJV).

God simplified everything. He says just be diligent do your part and leave the rest to me. But we have not believed and trusted in God for this help, instead we are exposing our children to the torment of the devil when we deny them to learn about God. They learned prayer in school.

If we want something good out of them, we must take the steps and endeavor to teach them what we believe is good and then sit back and wait for results, trusting God that the truth about what we taught will come out at some point. God is merciful, loving, and he cares for every one, so he dearly loves to see children become who he has created them to become. He, however, relies on us to be faithful and share (teach) with them what God intends for them.

We have a free will as human beings, which is to choose good or evil. Yet God in His sovereignty makes all avenues to see that we have been told the outcome of both good and evil.

Good is expected from children who have never been taught the source of good. If they can't say a prayer in school then we have doubted the power of prayer. They can't be good without the source of this good. Who among us became responsible, respectful to elders without being taught? Why do we think they are different? If we couldn't be good without being taught then they can't too. Look at what the Bible says about the children's hearts;

> Foolishness [is] bound in the heart of a child; [but] the rod of correction shall drive it far from him.
>
> Proverbs 22:15 KJV

The rod God talks about is spanking done reasonably to correct them. We might not need the spanking, especially when they are older but will instead need constant talking with us parents. We must correct our children; this should be done in love. For example, we have seen boys applying lipstick to look pretty like their mums or sisters. In their innocence we quickly conclude "My boy is gay, look at his lips." The right thing is to tell the kid(boy) that lipstick is for the girls and women for their beauty; men don't do that and we shall have saved their souls from the pressures.

The Bible says that what we sow is what we shall reap. It is not a good reaping presently in America, yet if we continue to sow carelessness and neglect toward our children, our harvest will be always so disappointing.

We decided that Bibles and other faith related issues should be separated from state. If teaching the Bible in schools is not misunderstood, this was one of the efficient and effective ways to preserve the next generations.

This opportunity should not be deprived from the children with the purpose of helping them know about God and how God has preserved this land. It is also an opportunity to let them choose what life they want to lead. It is impossible to expect good from someone who has never heard about good, yet evil surrounds them?

Let them have the opportunity to hear and learn about both. Then if he or she makes a decision, it is an informed decision, knowing the consequences of the kind of life he or she has chosen to lead.

It is so sad that good is expected from children who are surrounded by evil. It cannot be a wonder if they become what is surrounding them since it is ourselves, mums and dads, that are passionately supporting and practicing these evil ways.

Instead we have stood aside and claimed our children go to Christian schools so they are safe. These Christian schools will help them make good worthy decisions. Yes, this is true, but then we forget they have friends who do not go to Christian schools. Can their friends teach them what we avoided? They are their friends, and as children they will trust each other. What about if it's the children who attend Christian schools that teach the other ones that don't attend Christian schools? Yes, they can teach them, but it has not happened most of the time.

We have further forgotten that some of our neighbors' children do not go to Christian schools. Can we stop our children from having these neighbors' kids as friends? Many have tried to do this, but a few have been successful.

All these endeavors seem good for sure, yet we can do more for children and our neighbors' kids. We must begin to think of what we can do to help all of our kids, and there is something we can do. Let us give all the children a good foundation, and in this case not our children only, but our neighbors' too.

Let God be taught in schools, then we will have provided an avenue to let God have his way in the lives of all our children. From then on we shall not live in worry anymore about if we shall be able to raise our children safely, which has led to having one kid because he is manageable.

What harm did the Bibles do in schools? Could teaching the Bible be a simple issue and more achievable than the different strategies planned to fight crime?

Fighting crime goes hand-in-hand with understanding the cause of crime. From the chapter that follows we shall see that people can be normal and can be a problem as well depending on what influences there decision. Satan or God

The Bible is so powerful in that many countries in the world today are changed, peaceful, and prosperous because of the fear of God learned in schools.

The biggest percentage of the Bibles changing the world today are printed in America; yet us, who print the Bible have not been caring enough to ask why these changes seen in several countries are not what we see in our land.

In these very Bibles we read: "Train up a child in the way he should go, and when he is old he will not depart from it" (Proverbs 22:6, NKJV).

We are skeptical about Bibles taught in schools. So we ask ourselves this question:

How shall we be sure of what is to be taught will be true about God?

God asks us, "How old is the Bible, and who among us has lived to this day to see that the contents of the Bible have not changed?"

Because this is God's business, He will take care of it as He has always used someone to this day to preserve the contents of the Bible.

We further ask ourselves, won't this be a violation of the first amendment right?

God answers us. "I thought the idea of freedom in the first amendment right is inspired by the teachings from the Bible itself."

We have more questions: What about other books of the other religions?

God answers: "But this country is not like any other. I helped its founders who purposed to believe in the Bible."

We continue to ask: Isn't this a violation of rights?

God answers. "Rights are given by me if people don't know about me, then what rights do they have."

When all of our questions have been answered, the American people can now seek to reinstate the teaching of the Bible in schools.

Who has neglected the power of God from His Word? Apart from the one who says, "It is impossible to teach the Bible in schools," yet he gives no conclusive reason that God can't answer.

The decision to teach about God using the Bible in schools is not a new thing if we can remember that God is printed on the American dollar as "In God We Trust." This is the same God we are talking about.

Why was God above all things put on the currency (dollar)?

Who agreed to do that? If He is the God of the Bible, why not speak about Him in schools?

Why was this God trusted, and does this inscription on the dollar carry any meaning? Why can't the children learn about that God inscribed on the dollar? Aren't they missing something so special and important, and we can't forget that they are the future of the land. Without the help of the God trusted as inscribed on the dollar, the devil has set traps they can't overcome.

Who is left among us, the American people, to care about whether the children should learn about this inscription. It should be that we are here and we all care. After we agree to care, we have to prove to God, we mean it when we say we care because He is waiting to see how we shall show our care.

The future is all about what we do today. The fore fathers had this revelation from God's Word that what they wanted in the future today was to be done in their days. This was to teach their children and grandchildren so that the law wouldn't be forsaken in America.

School programs should accommodate Bible study in all schools if we are to secure the future of America by seeking to please God. Teaching the Bible in schools can be done at all levels of education. It is very possible; we can make this possible if we agree upon its benefits. Why is this possible to us especially? Because this is who we are; the things of God are easily understood by us the American people. It's a grace upon this land, and it's the solution to what we can presently deal with after sighting symptoms like greed, corruption, crime, and a change in morals among ourselves. The cause of all this has been lack of the fear of God, and this lack of fear of God can happen to anyone; no one is exceptional from it without putting God first in all that we do, falling of the track is so simple sometimes without our notice. From today the problem is not what has gone wrong anymore, we shouldn't worry but its how we shall respond to this message and caution from God.

God is waiting to see this happen soon as the most urgent need of the American people. It will be one of the signs of a country turning back to God.

If we can remember the people that have been innovative as we saw at the beginning of the chapter, yet American's future is not in the innovations growing across the country, minus acknowledging the giver of knowledge for these innovations. These good innovations can fail to achieve their purposes for discovery and can even be misused for evil purposes if the invention falls into the hands of corrupt, greedy, and careless-hearted people who can do anything with it that doesn't benefit the nation, but instead harms the nation and the world.

God is reminding us to be faithful, because our neglect of Him is so evident in the way our children live today. This only one act of faith can save the future of the American people. God is watching.

THE DEVIL'S PLAN

We have talked about the devil, also called Satan, all along and how he is interfering in what God plans to do with man. Let us specifically look at this devil and how he works, especially how he has invaded us in America. How can we know about the devil unless someone who knows him so well and knows how he works teaches us about him? This person who knows him so well is the Lord Jesus Christ, who was there in the beginning with God; all that he spoke was that he heard God speak as the Scripture says.

We should rely on the Word of God for understanding several things about our lives. Just as He promised that the Holy Spirit would show us all things in other words what was difficult to comprehend, we can know by the help of the Holy Spirit who dwells in us when we invite Jesus Christ in our lives as our Lord. The next chapter will be helpful about explaining all this.

From the above scripture however, we see Jesus Christ talk about Himself as speaking all that He hears His father (God) speak, so we believe Him when He tells us all things, even about the devil.

It's at the baptism of Jesus Christ that God first calls Jesus Christ His son.

> When He had been baptized, Jesus came up immediately from the water; and behold, the heavens were opened to Him, and He saw the Spirit of God descending like a dove and alighting upon Him. And suddenly a voice came from heaven, saying, "This is My beloved Son, in whom I am well pleased.
>
> Matthew 3:16-17 (NKJV)

Man is created in the image of God, but Satan has always come into the Spirit of man to defile the good nature of man. Just like when God relates with man it can lead man to be like God and the opposite is true If man is inspired by the devil, man can be so bad, and this is why the devil is so bad.

Satan influences man to sin against God, and this is true from God's Word, for the Bible says:

> He that committed sin is of the devil; for the devil sinned from the beginning. For this purpose, the Son of God was manifested, that he might destroy the works of the devil. Who so ever is born of God doth not commit sin; for his seed remained in him: and he cannot sin, because he is born of God.
>
> 1 John 3:8-9 (KJV)

Explaining to us that what makes man bad and why man must surrender to Jesus Christ for help if man is to survive and live a pure life, Jesus Christ came to set man free from evil, just as the Scriptures have mentioned. "The son of God, who is Jesus Christ was manifested to destroy the works of the devil," but also this answers the question, which has always been attached to our desire of being free: "Can man lead and control himself to being good?" The answer is no.

The devil influences man to hate God and hate fellow man. When we hate God, we can't love anyone, not even our spouses or children. Yet this is where the nation is headed. It sounds simple when someone says, "I don't love God," or, "I don't believe in God." Please, such a confession can be true about the person who speaks it, and of course they are free to speak that, but such confessions have a disastrous end.

America has desired freedom, saying, "I am not controlled by anyone. I control myself."

Meaning we want God out of the things we do, yet not knowing all that happens on the earth is God's business; He is the creator and our father. He cannot close His eyes and ears. He sees and He hears us as we suffer from the torments of the devil.

This is why He gave his only begotten son Jesus Christ to come and be punished in our place for our sins he who did not have any sin. We ought to realize that when Jesus died and rose from the dead, this was our victory as men and women. All it takes to part-take of this victory is accepting Jesus Christ in our lives. If man was able to control or lead himself in the proper path without the help of Jesus Christ, why did Jesus Christ then come?

As the Bible has said in 1 John 3:8–9, Jesus Christ came to destroy the works of the enemy, and if Jesus Christ is not leading, we are led by the one he came to destroy, who is the devil, Satan.

It sounds, unrealistic, untrue, and unsympathetic; it sounds unspiritual yet it is the truth. This further highlights why the study of the Word of God is important, we have been a round for some time yet some of these teaching have been neglected. Many truths in God's Word can sound just untrue like the truth we just read. God has put this in writing, the Bible for our understanding not to be offended in any way but that we shall learn about Him.

This is why all of us who want to be led by God must be saved by being born again through Jesus Christ, this is said by Jesus Christ himself and the only way he would help us.

Jesus answered and said to him, "Most assuredly, I say to you, unless one is born again, he cannot see the kingdom of God" (John 3:3, NKJV).

The devil looks for unbelief in our hearts and the things we are attracted to our selves to base his temptation. Let no one say when he is tempted, "I am tempted by God." For God cannot be tempted by evil; nor does He Himself tempt anyone. But each one is tempted when he is drawn away by his own desires and enticed. Then, when desire has conceived, it gives birth to sin; and sin, when it is full-grown, brings forth death. (James 1:13-15 NKJV)

For example, the devil tempts through ideas which come as inspirations, some sound to be brilliant ideas. This can begin in one person, spread to a family, continue to neighborhoods, to communities, continues nationwide, further across continent, and then to the whole world. So it doesn't matter how he does it by what age, level of education, power, or influence of someone; if not careful, we can be an instrument of the devil's plan. Realizing it is the devil's suggestion can be a problem, only through the word of God can we determine who inspires these suggestions in us many times we think we are doing something for the people but the motive behind it is inspired by the devil because it is done out of revenge, hatred, or fear.

When such evil things happen, it's proper to acknowledge wrong doing and repent of sins. Accept you're wrong and turn from evil ways and do what is pleasing in the sight of God.

We should note that not every thing a round us done by the people around us is true or right to do before God, we should be careful about what we copy from others. Can we find the source of what they are doing? If not, we must think twice. We in America are looking for something unique. Something that stands out, something brilliant, but all these mentioned categories can be possible enticing traps by the devil. It is not wrong to look for something unique because of the motive of promoting excellence, the challenge becomes where this uniqueness is from? What spirit is behind its inspiration before we take part in it or practice it?

How do we know that what we are doing is not from the devil or what we are saying is of God? We find the answer by asking ourselves individually, "What is the source of what we say or think or do? Is what we are doing from the Word of God or in line with the Word of God?" This means we must be students of the Word of God; otherwise, how shall we know our wrong if we don't stop to read the source of all correction, the Bible? It's the only standard to test whether what we do and say is evil or good.

The above is very important because many people in the world today are what they are because of what they have heard and seen not considering the source of these behaviors.

No matter what we have decided we want to be, it must be in line with God's Word. For the Bible is true and in it are the issues of this life.

We should consider doing what is godly, because we are all a precious creation of God and God knows what will bring us joy rather than when we are trapped into destruction as an individual and a nation.

Did we know that the day we distanced ourselves from Jesus Christ as a nation was the very time we allowed the devil to come into to everywhere. The devil occupies where the spirit of the LORD is not. It is supernatural, as we have seen above if Jesus Christ who was manifested to destroy the devil is not in, then the devil is still in and in total control.

The one we the American people allowed to come into our hearts and nation when we distanced ourselves form God by our actions, is our enemy and has never been good. No natural mind can see him or even discern the actions and deception of Satan. When he came in, he didn't introduce himself as "Satan," but silently he came in by our selves. We should not doubt he is in because of our own deeds. He can be in permanently if we don't work with God to show us how we can lose ourselves from him. We who began in faith are today in the fresh that every thing done is about us. It is about how we look before the rest of the world.

God trusted us to set the standards for the world in the way we lived. We were to set examples no matter what the world said about us. After sometime they would catch up with our way the godly way of course because God would prove to them our way was best for them to follow note; God would do that not we ourselves because every time we have done it in our strength we have failed. He has many ways to do it; many will be not our ways.

When we missed this to be the centre of how we operate, can we have any doubts that he (Satan) is in and inspiring his ways in form of false love that hides its evil motives in it's self. He has convinced us that God loves us but he is denying us the opportunity to love God and follow His Word. Only Jesus who was manifested to destroy him Satan will save us.

Instead America fight's the enemy's symptoms like crime, greedy, corruption, divorce, the rampant immorality rather than working to address the root and causes of these very symptoms. We are in the days where we are no longer patient about anything; such behavior is new in the land and was not heard of in the land. We want the American dream so quick just like that, it always took patience to achieve the dream. Americans worked with a heart to build the nation, help each other, work together, we where not to build personal empires, that's who we were. Today we are divided on every ground by every thing and its a trap, by Satan he has planed a wave of anger and hatred among ourselves.

We must begin working together, working for God first this leads to serving the people. If work is towards pleasing God we shall please men and if our efforts are about the people minus what God's opinion through His Word is, we are to become displeasing to God. Have we noticed that working for God implies focusing on where His eyes are, which are at the needs of our society. When He counsels us on long term solutions we should be willing to use them and reject Satan's quick ways of fixing problems. Satan causes the problems and inspires quick random solutions that continue to worsen our problems. If we show we are in sincere need of God's help through our change of life and minds, He is going to help.

Note that God helps those that invite him for help and He does it only through Jesus Christ.

Not those that help themselves because if they can help themselves why need the help of God? For example, the world knows he exists but we don't recognize Him in our lives, this is the disobedience influenced by Satan. This why from this understanding He helps those that honor Him and live a life that respects Him. His being silent doesn't mean He doesn't see and know. He looks for people to work with but many times we shy away when He calls on us. Are we The American People going to be the people He is looking for? A people that honor Him? A loving people? A forgiving people? A people who know this life is so short so we should use it to our best ability in honor to God other than live in short lived pleasure and forever be tormented in Hell with Satan.

Note again; that we are not working together any more to achieve common purpose, and this is every where from homes between mum and dad to the offices within all levels of the organization, people rival on all things, how can we achieve any success? Such is not what this land is all about. America has missed the point and things going wrong will prove that because these are the very plans of the devil.

For example we are so diverse yet we used to have something in common: the worship of God. If the enemy is attacking this one thing that joins us, big trouble a waits us.

America's unity has a whole has well laid out purpose which is entirely attached to the American soil, and, minus God, then everything will fall apart. Just take time to think about the world empires that are now remembered or even not remembered anymore, These were so powerful for a purpose and without purpose they lost it all .And no matter the different causes in which they lost it, it was the devil's cause for their failures. The devil plans the exact failure for America, and although it may seem so impossible to us, without the change in our lives, we have seen what can happen.

Books have been written about the rise and fall of super powers. God is cautioning us that this is not very far from happening to America, where books can be written about the great fallen American empire with titles, "The Rise and Fall." This is what the devil plans. He has persuaded America to shift to a false freedom that encourages sin,this' is different from the freedom of God, which is to be free of sin. The devil wishes and has planned shame on America.

Jesus said: "The thief cometh not, but for to steal, and to kill, and to destroy: I am come that they might have life, and that they might have [it] more abundantly" (John 10:10, KJV).

Jesus says for this the devil can't come, except to steal, to kill, and destroy. The devil has got several ways on how to fulfill his mission. The devil is not afraid of anyone. God desires that this would be understood; as man we forget this all the time. The devil can tempt anybody and can use anyone. Even the one we respect in society, respect in governments, even in the places of worship, for the devil can use highly respected people to fulfill his mission of stealing, killing, and destroying.

So ask Jesus Christ to come into our lives to give us authority to discern the devil's temptations and not yield to them. Jesus Christ comes to give back what was taken away from man; the relationship with God, when the Holy Spirit comes to live in us. This will result in relating with God, which will result in the power to say no to sin and the ability to obey when God speaks to us. This means life without Jesus Christ can be so disappointing, full of trouble, and meaningless.

THE STATE OF THE AMERICAN INDIVIDUAL

God desires the best for every one of us, although he has one concern about us as individuals. He is concerned about our inability to remember that in this world we are born with nothing and so shall live with nothing yet this understanding doesn't reflect in the way we live as individuals.

As individuals we worry about life that life becomes uncomfortable for ourselves and the people around us. Our worry has come to the point where it now doesn't matter how we live, how we treat others or what we do, as long as we quench our worry. We are completely looking in wrong directions for answers.

We forget that God has good plans for every one of us, this confirmation is seen in the way he spoke to the children of Israel promising them a good land.

In His promise, He also warned them to keep his commandments as a concern; otherwise all that they desired was to be available in the Promised Land. This warning and His concerns apply to us this day being that we know God is the same yesterday today and forever.

This was the promise and concern of God when he spoke to the children of Israel;

> Therefore you shall keep the commandments of the LORD your God to walk in his ways and to fear him. For the LORD your God is bringing you into a good land or land of brooks of water, of fountains and springs, that flow out of valleys and hills. A land of wheat and barley of vines and fig trees and pomegranates, a land of olive oil and honey. A land in which you will eat bread without scarcity, in which you will lack nothing a land whose stones are iron and out of whose hills you can dig copper.
>
> Deuteronomy 8:16 (NKJV)

Remember this was the promise of God to the children of Israel as they prepared themselves to enter the promised Land. What is so special about this scripture and promise is that this scripture defines the present-day America? In its fullness, we are witnesses that the promised land given to the fore fathers is evident today just like the one God was telling the children of Israel.

Although God wants man to live in a good land, live in plenty without scarcity as we noted above. He is also concerned about the way man lives to the end of his life, which is being a godly person. God's plan was and is still about a relationship with us men and women the people he created. His plan for us individually, is that we become a people who are willing to ask for His will to be on earth as it is in heaven and be able to work the will of God out as we relate to fellow men and women with love and care, in truth, mercy, and justice. All of this is what God planned and we could individually do.

God continued to caution them in Deuteronomy 8:10-1 through Moses and said, "When you have eaten and are full, then you shall bless the LORD your God for the good which he has given you."

We have eaten, gotten full but have forgotten to bless the LORD our God for the good which he has given us, instead we have denied His help in all ways just as the many ways we looked at in the previous chapters.

Jesus Christ, who came to teach us about what is important in life as individuals, told this to his disciples who worried about life.

Then one from the crowd said to Him, "Teacher, tell my brother to divide the inheritance with me."

But He said to him, "Man, who made Me a judge or an arbitrator over you?" And He said to them, "Take heed and beware of covetousness, for one's life does not consist in the abundance of the things he possesses." Then He spoke a parable to them, saying: "The ground of a certain rich man yielded plentifully. And he thought within himself, saying, 'What shall I do, since I have no room to store my crops?' So he said, 'I will do this: I will pull down my barns and build greater, and there I will store all my crops and my goods. And I will say to my soul, "Soul, you have many goods laid up for many years; take your ease; eat, drink, *and* be merry."' But God said to him, 'Fool! This night your soul will be required of you; then whose will those things be which you have provided?'

"So *is* he who lays up treasure for himself, and is not rich toward God."

How was this man not rich towards God? He invested, he worked hard to get all he had, yet in all this God knew he was to look for those in need and feed them. What would he loose for he had plenty.

Jesus continued;

Then He said to His disciples, "Therefore I say to you, do not worry about your life, what you will eat; nor about the body, what you will put on. Life is more than food, and the body *is more* than clothing. Consider the ravens, for they neither sow nor reap, which have neither storehouse nor barn; and God feeds them. Of how much more value are you than the birds? And which of you by worrying can add one cubit to his stature? If you then are not able to do *the* least, why are you anxious for the rest? Consider the lilies, how they grow: they neither toil nor spin; and yet I say to you, even Solomon in all his glory was not arrayed like one of these. If then God so clothes the grass, which today is in the field and tomorrow is thrown into the oven, how much more *will He clothe* you, O *you* of little faith?

"And do not seek what you should eat or what you should drink, nor have an anxious mind. For all these things the nations of the world seek after, and your Father knows that you need these things. But seek the kingdom of God, and all these things shall be added to you.

"Do not fear, little flock, for it is your Father's good pleasure to give you the kingdom. Sell what you have and give alms; provide yourselves money bags which do not grow old, a treasure in the heavens that does not fail, where no thief approaches nor moth destroys. For where your treasure is, there your heart will be also. (Luke 12:22-34 NKJV)

We have sought for knowledge and unders-tanding in many ways and have missed on some of these profound truth about life. We're missing on how God views us individually. Jesus Christ knew these things so He taught them, as a command from his father because what he heard his father (God) say, he said and did also. According to God, if we shall seek to attain His kingdom, we shall have succeeded because this is the most important of all things. Where our treasure will be there our hearts will be also, where have we put our treasures as individuals?

Jesus explains how riches and pleasures can be so deceptive in another parable of the rich man, He shows us that out of fear and worry we have acted un knowingly towards selfishness which will cost us our prize, the everlasting happiness in heaven.

> There was a certain rich man who was clothed in purple and fine linen and fared sumptuously every day. But there was a certain beggar named Lazarus, full of sores, who was laid at his gate, desiring to be fed with the crumbs which fell from the rich man's table. Moreover the dogs came and licked his sores. So it was that the beggar died, and was carried by the angels to Abraham's bosom. The rich man also died and was buried. And being in torments in Hades, he lifted up his eyes and saw Abraham afar off, and Lazarus in his bosom.
>
> Then he cried and said, "Father Abraham, have mercy on me, and send Lazarus that he may dip the tip of his finger in water and cool my tongue; for I am tormented in this flame." But Abraham said, "Son, remember that in your lifetime you received your good things, and likewise Lazarus evil things; but

> now he is comforted and you are tormented. And besides all this, between us and you there is a great gulf fixed, so that those who want to pass from here to you cannot, nor can those from there pass to us."
>
> Then he said, "I beg you therefore, father, that you would send him to my father's house, for I have five brothers, that he may testify to them, lest they also come to this place of torment." Abraham said to him, "They have Moses and the prophets; let them hear them." And he said, "No, father Abraham; but if one goes to them from the dead, they will repent." But he said to him, "If they do not hear Moses and the prophets, neither will they be persuaded though one rise from the dead."
>
> (Luke 16:19-31 NKJV)

We attach having money to being blessed by God, but the story shows it's very possible to be rich and so successful and go to Hell. Like it can be very possible to be so poor and go to Hell too. We should consider the source of our wealth and consider how we use our wealth individually. From the story the rich man had his share, which he enjoyed here on earth, so he had no more portion in heaven; instead, his was in hell. On the other hand the poor man suffered on earth but stayed right before God, and so he deserved enjoying in heaven. Not only do we see this but we also find answers to the questions that have always troubled us. Questions like; what happens to the ones that leave this life without having pleased God? Does Hell really exist? Is Heaven the only place after this life? Can people cross from Hell because their sin will be reduced depending on how we pray for their souls? Is forgiveness received in this life only or we can get forgiveness after this life on earth?

We can get answers to our questions from this parable; as Jesus said; when we leave this life without having received forgiveness, we have no other opportunity; because from the parable Abraham said to the rich man when he cried for help; "Son, remember that in your lifetime you received your good things, and likewise Lazarus evil things; but now he is comforted and you are tormented. And besides all this, between us and you there is a great gulf fixed, so that those who want to pass from here to you cannot, nor can those from there pass to us." We should then seek to please God as bottom-line otherwise we have a limited time.

God believes in us as individuals, He knows when we read and learn about Him through his Word we shall be obedient. This is, however, the opposite when we say we don't need to give that attention to the Bible, since we know and love God, yet we hide our hearts far from him, proven by the way we individually live (life style). For example, we have loved pets more than our neighbors, friends, and relatives. Marriages have been broken, because one doesn't understand the way the other is not used to pets, and relationships have collapsed. Do we care for pets more than we can care for our parents, care for our relatives, care for those that sit in the same rooms with us in our places of work, places of worship, those in our communities. What about how we can care for the people who have helped us become who we are today as individuals? If marriages have been broken, because one of the spouses doesn't understand how the other is not used to pets have pets become so important?

Leading to disagreements that have collapsed good relationships. Is it wrong to love pets or even keep them? No, it is not wrong, but is it right to love and care for pets more than we love and care for fellow man created in the image of God? No, it is not good either.

Of course, no one should regulate what we do with what we have. Instead let us remind ourselves that what we have is from God. It's an opportunity to have what we have, so let us be thankful to Him by honoring Him with our possessions when we show our love and care by helping our parents, neighbors, relatives, workmates, and all those in need.

The word of God says; "Honor the LORD with thy substance and with the first fruits of all thine increase" (Proverbs 3:9, KJV).

God wanted the American people to be good examples, to be self-sufficient as he desires for the rest of the world, so he gave us a land full of minerals, as the scripture explains. Instead we have decided to look elsewhere for supplies, pushing ourselves to dependency and in the end we are in lack. It is though our land is barren. By this we have desired to depend on others, yet God made us independent when the forefathers came to the land. It is sinful for us to make the land impossible for life. Where else shall we run to for help if this land is to become impossible? America, as a land, is a good land. We must ask God to show us how this land can still sustain us as we do more research on the land. Otherwise it's painful to depend, yet we have so many of us that are willing to work. The land has everything as the Scriptures said.

The problem is not that the land has all of a sudden become nonproductive with no minerals at all. The challenge is that we have not individually been able to take heed of the Word of God. We are therefore failing to see how the land is good. God warned about our behavior the same the behavior that causes our eyes not see the goodness of the Land. He said;

> Lest when you have eaten and are full and have built beautiful houses and dwell in them and when your herds and your flocks multiply and your silver and your gold multiplied and all that you have is multiplied. When your heart is lifted up and you forget the Lord your God who

> brought you out of the land of Egypt
> from house of bondage.
>
> Deuteronomy 8:12-13 (NKJV)

This scripture is saying today America's flocks are multiplied, our silver and our gold are multiplied; all that we have is multiplied. When our hearts have been lifted up by becoming happy about how much we have achieved instead we have forgotten the LORD our God who brought our forefathers out of Europe, the house of bondage to the new land as history has it.

Saying our hard work has gained us what we have, we forget God warned about this very issue in" (Deuteronomy 8:17, NKJV). Saying; then you say in your heart, "My power and the might of my hand have gained me this wealth."

God is telling us that; "You shall remember the LORD your God, for it is he who gives you power to get wealth, for one reason, that he may establish his covenant which he swore to your fathers as it is this day" (Deuteronomy 8:18, NKJV).

God swore to our fathers as it is this day, and this wealth will be lost if it loses its purpose, as the Word has said. Let us honor God and help others know God so that they will honor him too.

We should be the first people to honor him in our lives then be an example to the world. This is the most important purpose of the individual's and the nation's wealth. This is why America is wealthy as a nation. It is sin if we under play the lives and ways of the forefathers, by assuming they were like any other people without the fear and love for God. If it where so, America would have been a different country altogether. Who knows no one of us would be here.

The above cautions were carefully understood and practiced by America's forefathers. They are worth paying attention to, because God explains how we, the American people, can perish: "Then it shall be, if you by any means forget the LORD your God, and follow other Gods and serve them and worship them, you shall surely perish" (Deuteronomy 8:19, KJV).

Just as God said it then, the same way it applies today that if we follow other gods and serve them, America will be no more. We shall perish. We must open our physical and spiritual eyes and ears to all the things happening around us they seem to be working towards this very end, destruction.This is no matter how they are happening without our return to the true love of God which is expressed in our actions, we are gone.Only God can save us from all this division among our selves.

We are fulfilling the devil's plans and falling into his trap, like we saw; the devil wants us to be ignorant of this truth; this is why at times we feel offended by what is truth. Yet it's this truth that can heal our broken hearts and, in the end, heal our land. We forget that this life is so short at 120 years, and it's in these few years that we must make the decision which will determine our life forever. We now know this as seen in the parable of Lazarus and the rich man. Remember the LORD said, "My Spirit shall not strive with man forever, for he is indeed flesh; yet his days shall be one hundred and twenty years" (Genesis 6:3, NKJV). God gave these years as limits and we must have the best use of our time on earth. Why should we be so taken up? Jesus says:

> "If anyone desires to come after Me, let him deny himself, and take up his cross, and follow Me. For whoever desires to save his life will lose it, but whoever loses his life for My sake

> will find it. For what profit is it to a man if he gains the whole world, and loses his own soul? Or what will a man give in exchange for his soul? For the Son of Man will come in the glory of His Father with His angels, and then He will reward each according to his works.
>
> (Matthew 16:24-27 NKJV)

In all this God is still speaking to us individually in love He says; and you have forgotten the exhortation which speaks to you as to sons:

"My son, do not despise the chastening of the LORD. Nor be discouraged when you are rebuked by Him for whom the LORD loves He chastens, and scourges every son whom He receives."

If we endure chastening, God deals with us as with sons; for what son is there whom a father does not chasten? (Hebrews 12:5-7 NKJV) If we are without chastening, we would look at all this message as a violation of our right to be free, then we are illegitimate and not sons. Furthermore, we have had human fathers who corrected us, and we paid them respect. Shall we not much more readily be in subjection to the Father of spirits and live?

The will of God for America is that we individually use the wealth and freedom in America; not to become haters of God and do the lusts of our hearts. But that we do what pleases God. The forefathers believed God, for this was the freedom from sin: freedom to worship, freedom to serve God, freedom to love God, freedom to live a life pleasing before God, freedom to renounce every work of Satan within us by becoming true believers; accepting Jesus Christ as our personal LORD and Savior, and allowing God to change us from the sinful nature of man and live a pure life.

God wants us to change from a sinful life, because this is not what he created us to be but also because the wages of sin is death. "For the wages of sin is death, but the gift of God is eternal life in Christ Jesus our LORD" (Romans 6:23, NKJV).

This will not change, and if we are to avoid death, we must be willing to change. God is not going to change the punishment to the devil. Did the devil ask for forgiveness? He instead plans to take all of us if possible with him into his punishment if we stay disobedient to God. Watch because today the devil is using several platforms to trap us into his punishment. Yet it's we, men and women, who must change from sin to accept the forgiveness of God and escape punishment with the devil.

Sin has been turned into a joking matter in America. Do we talk about sin anymore? We are afraid of being called spiritual? So we don't associate with godliness at all, unless we are in our places of worship or if its our day of worship. We have misused the grace of God to do all sorts of evil. Please, God loves everybody, every sinner, but he is limited to what he can do if we decide not to be forgiven through Jesus Christ who died to pay a price for our sins, that we should not be punished in hell for our shortcomings. If we believe in him (Jesus Christ) individually, and begin to live as his word is, then we will be saved.

"For God so loved the world, that he gave his only begotten Son, that whosoever believe in him should not perish, but have everlasting life" (John 3:16).

If we fail to understand this or even not explain it in its simplicity, we have failed God and the land has just missed and lost its purpose.

People were to come to America to learn about God. They were to change from false beliefs, and escape the devil's traps that are manifested through false prophets who have encouraged killing of fellow men in pursuit of heaven. To God such acts can't lead to Heaven instead they are in the way leading to eternal torment with the devil.

For America, God purposed for a land and a people who would individually be zealous for true worship through Jesus Christ, a land which would have individuals as the most knowledgeable people about God's will and the Bible. Such individuals were to shine in their communities, schools, work places, shine in leadership positions guiding each other to forsake anything that makes us disobedient to God.

While in America, change was to be a gradual process, slowly through the love showed to them, they would see the love of God which would lead to their relationship with the land's true living God and His son Jesus Christ. This was and is still one of God's plans; minus this, we the American people have failed God.

For a long time now the devil is asking God whether we the American people deserve to live in plenty and why not suffer and lack like the rest of the world since we are turning away from God. Its only through Jesus Christ that we still live because of the hope God has in us. Yet we ask Why Jesus

Christ is important? Can't we love God without Jesus? The answer is No. For God to see who among us people would joke about His name in everything they did. He sent Jesus Christ to come and be born among man live with us and show us the thoughts of God, his works are still the standard for any person that has or will ever mention about knowing and believing in God. God planed that if we individually said we knew God we had to know Jesus Christ and do what he said and taught. Through Jesus Christ we now know and see the mind and the nature of God. This is why knowing and loving God without Jesus Christ doesn't exist.

Let this mind be in you which was also in Christ Jesus, who, being in the form of God, did not consider it robbery to be equal with God, but made Himself of no reputation, taking the form of a bondservant, and coming in the likeness of men. And being found in appearance as a man, He humbled Himself and became obedient to the point of death, even the death of the cross. Therefore God also has highly exalted Him and given Him the name which is above every name, that at the name of Jesus, every knee should bow, of those in heaven, and of those on earth, and of those under the earth, and that every tongue should confess that Jesus Christ is LORD, to the glory of God the Father. (Philippians 2: 5-11 NKJV)

Like to the whole world God puts Jesus Christ before us so that we shall follow him and be judged by his Word through Jesus Christ

God has stayed faithful and is giving us a reminder with an opportunity to repent, waiting to see how we shall act after we read this message.

We the inhabitants were to lift up Jesus Christ by bearing the fruits of the spirit and letting our light to shine through love for each other.

This is what failed in Europe among other things, so the forefathers crossed from there to America to do the Word and will of the LORD. When they came, they created ways to stay focused on their reason for coming. Now that they are gone, we have not bothered about them and have only remembered them in photos and monuments, all over the cities and museums also remembering them through celebrations every year.

They had reasons; one was to love. This is when people of all religions joined them here. Very importantly, as Christians they knew this love is the only way to show that they were disciples of Jesus.

A new commandment I give to you, that you love one another; as I have loved you, that you also love one another. By this all will know that you are My disciples, if you have love for one another" (John 13:34-35, NKJV).

What has happened today is that there is no love among us. We only love in pursuit of our individual hidden a genders. We are up to gaining individual fame, respect and power. This life and mindset has followed to our homes, schools and communities which according to Satan will lead to the next generations being even more disobedient to God. Even in the places of worship themselves, we are divided about cheap things, issues about who knows about God more than the other? Instead we are pointing fingers at each other, speaking about each other. Creating a society that largely talks about God but do not have Him as priority. We are a Christian nation but what kind of Christians are we?

God looks at us individually and wonders how far we are going away from Him when we suppose that we know Him, but failing to be one body and do His Word in love. It will be such a disappointment having done all we say we do for

God and the people yet to God it's in disobedience and therefore in vain.

This has made Christianity of no effect, so that Christians have changed to doing things unthinkable. We are Christians, yet we don't follow the teachings of Jesus Christ any more. God was our all in all, yet today, because of the life we must live called "success" we are only about the money, attached to everything and this money has become our all in all. What is wrong with money? There is nothing wrong with money but can we suspend being what God has created us to be because of money? It shouldn't be worth it.

God sees all this, wondering how far we are to go with all this worry upon us, He is calling us back to our first love, the love we had toward Him through our love for others and the hate we had for Sin.

Jesus Christ warned us too when He said; "Take heed and beware of covetousness, for one's life does not consist in the abundance of the things he possesses'" (Luke 12:15, NKJV). The things we have put our trust in are all going to pass away.

Jesus Christ teaches about what has taken his place in our hearts today, saying,

Heaven and earth will pass away, but My words will by no means pass away. But of that day and hour no one knows, not even the angels of heaven, but My Father only. But as the days of Noah were, so also will the coming of the Son of Man be. For as in the days before the flood, they were eating and drinking, marrying and giving in marriage, until the day that Noah entered the ark, and did not know until the flood came and took them all away, so also will the coming of the Son of Man be. Then two men will be in the field: one will be taken and the other left. Two women will be grinding at the mill: one will be taken and the other left. Watch therefore, for you do not know what hour your LORD is coming. But know this, that if the master of the house had known what hour the thief would come, he would have watched and not allowed his house to be broken into. Therefore you also be ready, for the Son of Man

> is coming at an hour you do not expect. Who then is a faithful and wise servant, whom his master made ruler over his household, to give them food in due season? Blessed is that servant whom his master, when he comes, will find so doing. Assuredly, I say to you that he will make him ruler over all his goods. But if that evil servant says in his heart, 'My master is delaying his coming,' and begins to beat his fellow servants, and to eat and drink with the drunkards, the master of that servant will come on a day when he is not looking for him and at an hour that he is not aware of, and will cut him in two and appoint him his portion with the hypocrites. There shall be weeping and gnashing of teeth.
>
> Matthew 24:35-51(NKJV)

We say we love, but how can we love each other if we can't trust each other, and how shall this build the kingdom of God? Success in the kingdom of

God is not determined by how great we become or how famous we are or by the following. What gain is it then if we are known by the whole world yet our names are not written in the book of life? The kingdom of God mindset we ought to have is about how many people we help to become great as we are, and this is in all the aspects of life. We look at the life of Jesus Christ before going to heaven; he transformed many into becoming just like him to the extent that they were called Christians which means "just like Christ or Christ like" and to this day the gospel is taught and preached. That is called success.

This applies not only to the gospel, but to all the other spheres like in business, family, Leadership and community. Success should be determined by how many we have inspired, taught, helped, guided, or mentored, so that they can exactly do what we are doing when we are gone, and this is in honor of God. So that even when we diversify and begin to do something else the ones we mentored, inspired are able to do everything without us, this is how enlargement comes to us. Jesus Christ is a good example; he showed us the kingdom of God by his actions. We should not lose hope. Let us be glad because we can ask the kingdom of God to come on earth as it is in heaven (Matthew 6: 9-13).

If Jesus comes back, what will happen to all that we are piling up for ourselves? Yet need is all around us, in our churches, temples, synagogues, and the neighborhoods themselves, before we look too far.

The devil has turned the American people into modern Christians, the ones who say, "Love God, but don't follow the teachings of Jesus Christ." We say, "God is love, and merciful. "There is no punishment for sin. Be what you want to be" Love God without his Word the Bible. We have said there are many ways to God." When we say or believe this, we are not Christians. Since Christians cannot be Christians without Christ. The word Christian itself is from Christ as we noted above. We cannot know about Christianity without the Bible. The Bible showed us God and Christ; only from the Bible can we know God and Christ.

The devil Satan has turned the land to that one where people from everywhere with sinful ideas can come to and practice freely and even teach them to others. Of course they don't force anyone, but our own search for peace and joy in wrong directions leads us into these traps. Without individually considering, understanding, and practicing the Bible, our world will be no more. God is well aware that we have kept questioning when Jesus will come back. In our efforts to discourage the ones that warn us about the punishment in Hell supposing we die with out repentance. Here he gives us the answer: "But the heavens and the earth which are now preserved by the same word, are reserved for fire until the Day of Judgment and perdition of ungodly men.

But, beloved, do not forget this one thing, that with the LORD one day is as a thousand years, and a thousand years as one day. The LORD is not slack concerning His promise, as some count slackness, but is long suffering toward us, not willing that any should perish but that all should come to repentance" (2 Peter 3:7-9 NKJV) He is waiting for us to repent.

Without faith it is impossible to please God. While "faith comes by hearing, hearing by the word of God" (Romans 10:17, NKJV), yet the Word of God says Jesus Christ is "the way, the truth, and the life. No one can see the father except through him" (John 14:6, NKJV).

When the forefathers believed God, they accepted Jesus Christ. This made all the difference.

Isaiah proclaimed in chapter sixty-one verse one who Jesus was, while in Luke 4:18, Jesus says about himself, "The spirit of the LORD is upon me, because he has anointed me to preach the gospel to the poor. He has sent me to heal the brokenhearted. To preach deliverance to the captives. And recovery of sight to the blind. To set at liberty those who are oppressed to preach the acceptable year of the LORD."

Let these reasons for Jesus' coming be manifested within our lives individually and corporately as a country. All that Jesus came for can be accomplished in our life today if we choose to surrender our lives to the Prince of Peace.

We should want to prolong our days; we should want it to be well with us, well with our lives, well with our jobs, well with our finances, well with our spouses, well with our children, well with our family, well with our leaderships, our responsibilities, and the many aspects of our lives. This is good and our desires for all these issues have no problem.

Jesus answered and said to them, "Those who are well have no need of a physician, but those who are sick. I have not come to call the righteous, but sinners, to repentance." (Luke 5:31-32 NKJV)

Jesus Christ loves a broken and contrite heart; a repentant heart. Being repentant is acknowledging sin in your life and asking for forgiveness. If we believe God is holy, how can we doubt He doesn't tolerate non repentant people? Lets be of good courage. He will forgive us and change us when we ask and believe in Jesus Christ instead of covering up our sin.

We have been taken on a ride to believe that Jesus Christ doesn't care about how we live and what we do. The spirit behind that message is the antichrist Spirit that doesn't acknowledge the saving power of Christ. The Bible warned about this spirit;

> Little children, it is the last hour; and as you have heard that the Antichrist is coming, even now many antichrists have come, by which we know that it is the last hour. They went out from us, but they were not of us; for if they had been of us, they would have continued with us; but they went out

> that they might be made manifest,
> that none of them were of us.
>
> (1John 2:18-19 NKJV)

It's a lie to think we can just live in every evil imaginations because Jesus isn't concerned, we don't know the time or hour when He will come back to judge the world. We should be prepared, he will come like a thief in the night as written in 2 Peter 3:10.

Remember Jesus Christ lived with many that were referred to by others as sinners; they were sinners because of their actions which were contrary to their faith, it's true, but they accepted Jesus into their lives, and the words of Jesus set them free. The prostitutes, drunkards, and tax collectors all followed as a symbol of a change of life, but also didn't do any of these things again as evidence of a changed life. If Jesus doesn't care about sin, how come He warns about hell? This is evidence of how important heaven is to Jesus Christ, than being silent and achieve honor from man.

> Then the scribes and Pharisees brought to Him a woman caught

in adultery. And when they had set her in the midst, they said to Him, "Teacher, this woman was caught in adultery, in the very act. Now Moses, in the law, commanded us that such should be stoned. But what do You say?" This they said, testing Him, that they might have something of which to accuse Him. But Jesus stooped down and wrote on the ground with His finger, as though He did not hear.

So when they continued asking Him, He raised Himself up and said to them, "He who is without sin among you, let him throw a stone at her first." And again He stooped down and wrote on the ground. Then those who heard it, being convicted by their conscience, went out one by one, beginning with the oldest even to the last. And Jesus was left alone, and the woman standing in the midst. When Jesus had raised Himself up and saw no one but the woman, He said to her, "Woman,

> where are those accusers of yours? Has no one condemned you?"
>
> She said, "No one, Lord."
>
> And Jesus said to her, "Neither do I condemn you; go and[k] sin no more."
>
> Then Jesus spoke to them again, saying, "I am the light of the world. He who follows Me shall not walk in darkness, but have the light of life.
>
> John 8:3-12 (NKJV)

Note that Jesus tells her: "Neither do I condemn you; go and sin no more." If Jesus Christ didn't care about sin as we say today, why does He warn her about sinning no more? He could have said, "Sorry, these people are demonizing your life, you were created like that, I love you as you are just follow me, these who brought you don't know, God is love." No He didn't tell her this. The trouble is when we say we have not sinned or when we say it doesn't matter what we do God loves us the way we are and fail to see that the reason He loves us is to forgive us our sins through Jesus when we admit we have sin. The point is that we shouldn't give up about asking God to change us and we know God will help if we are willing to acknowledge sin. God warns us individually to watch what we say and what we have been told when we think we defend our sin as a way of life calling it inevitable. Haven't we read Therefore let him who thinks he stands take heed lest he fall. No temptation has overtaken you except such as is common to man; but God is faithful, who will not allow you to be tempted beyond what you are able, but with the temptation will also make the way of escape, that you may be able to bear it. (1 Corinthians 10:12-13 NKJV) How big are our temptations? Its a reminder and caution to all of us.

Only acknowledge sin and ask for forgiveness from God through Jesus Christ. All that keeps us away from God is all vanity nothing substantial is in it. Jesus Christ is waiting to come into your life first, so that you will receive the Holy Spirit, who will enable you to resist the influence of the devil from your life.

Since you will receive Jesus Christ in your life, you will introduce him to your family, school, work place and community. They will all see how you have changed. They will desire what is in you, this is the Will of God. Remember repentance is individual. Jesus Christ is a personal savior.

You can believe in Jesus Christ. Even as you read this portion of God's message, you will receive salvation so that you can live a free life that pleases God. God wants to guide you through this way because you have never been there, or you have but stumbled sometimes. Don't be troubled. Today, Jesus Christ gives new mercies for you to overcome.

Confess and believe these following words in faith to accept Jesus Christ in your life today.

> Have mercy upon me, O God,
>   According to Your
> loving kindness;
>   According to the multitude
> of Your tender mercies,
>   Blot out my transgressions.
>   Wash me thoroughly
> from my iniquity,
>   And cleanse me from my sin.
>   For I acknowledge
> my transgressions,
>   And my sin is always before me.
>   Against You, You only,
> have I sinned,
>   And done this evil in Your sight—

That You may be found
just when You speak,
And blameless when You judge.
Behold, I was brought
forth in iniquity,
And in sin my mother
conceived me.
Behold, You desire truth
in the inward parts,
And in the hidden part You
will make me to know wisdom.
Purge me with hyssop,
and I shall be clean;
Wash me, and I shall
be whiter than snow.
Make me hear joy and gladness,
That the bones You have
broken may rejoice.
Hide Your face from my sins,
And blot out all my iniquities.
Create in me a clean
heart, O God,
And renew a steadfast
spirit within me.
Do not cast me away
from Your presence,

And do not take Your
Holy Spirit from me.
Restore to me the joy
of Your salvation,
And uphold me by
Your generous Spirit.
Then I will teach
transgressors Your ways,
And sinners shall be
converted to You.
Deliver me from the guilt
of bloodshed, O God,
The God of my salvation,
And my tongue shall sing
aloud of Your righteousness.
O LORD, open my lips,
And my mouth shall
show forth Your praise.
For You do not desire sacrifice,
or else I would give it;
You do not delight
in burnt offering.
The sacrifices of God
are a broken spirit,
A broken and a contrite heart—

These, O God, You
will not despise.
Do good in Your good
pleasure to Zion;
Build the walls of Jerusalem.
Then You shall be pleased with
the sacrifices of righteousness,
With burnt offering and
whole burnt offering;
Then they shall offer
bulls on Your altar.

Psalm 51:1 (NKJV)

Jesus, from now on I accept you as my LORD and savior. I believe you are the son of God; you died and rose and now you live in heaven. In Jesus' mighty name I pray. Amen.

The words you just proclaimed in faith have set you free, so you are free. God has forgiven your sins. "For there is now no more condemnation for those in Christ Jesus" (Romans 1:1, NKJV).

Who in this world would be saved if salvation had to be paid for? Salvation is here for everyone tell some one about it. Heaven rejoices about only one repenting to follow Jesus as LORD and savior, Jesus said; "what woman, having ten silver coins if she loses one coin, does not light a lamp, sweep the house, and search carefully until she finds it? And when she has found it, she calls her friends and neighbors together, saying, 'Rejoice with me, for I have found the piece which I lost!' Likewise, I say to you, there is joy in the presence of the angels of God over one sinner who repents." (Luke 15:8-10 NKJV)

A miracle has just happened. Romans 10:8-10

> The word is near you, even in your mouth and in your heart (that is the word of faith which we preach) that if you confess with your mouth the LORD Jesus and believe in your heart that God has raised him from the dead, you will be saved. For with the heart man believes to righteousness; and with the mouth confession is made to salvation.

For the Scripture says, whoever believes on Him will not be put to shame. By the confession you made, you have decided to accept the freedom due to you, by renouncing the devil and his works. This is who you are, a people of freedom. Not freedom as given in the world, but freedom not to sin against God and being free to serve God in truth and spirit. Find a church, synagogue, or temple in your community and tell the brethren that you are a now a new creation; the old has gone and the new has come. Tell them you have made a choice to follow Jesus Christ and you would want to learn more about God.

This is who we are, free individually and free as a nation. America, servants of God, for this is what makes the difference, and this was the American dream for our forefathers. "God bless America and God save America. Amen."

THE FUTURE OF AMERICA

As times become tougher, God has continued to open doors for us, providing an escape from the devil's traps. God sees and knows, and His plans never change, for His plans are to give America a good and peaceful life, as He plans for the rest of the world. This is why we should know this truth, because these are the last days, as evident in Jesus's teaching when, if not careful, we shall doubt the love of God for us.

> Now as He sat on the Mount of Olives, the disciples came to Him privately, saying, "Tell us, when will these things be? And what will be the sign of Your coming, and of the end of the age?"

And Jesus answered and said to them: "Take heed that no one deceives you. For many will come in My name, saying, 'I am the Christ,' and will deceive many. And you will hear of wars and rumors of wars. See that you are not troubled; for all these things must come to pass, but the end is not yet. For nation will rise against nation, and kingdom against kingdom. And there will be famines, pestilences, and earthquakes in various places. All these are the beginning of sorrows.

"Then they will deliver you up to tribulation and kill you, and you will be hated by all nations for My name's sake. And then many will be offended, will betray one another, and will hate one another. Then many false prophets will rise up and deceive many. And because lawlessness will abound, the love of many will grow cold. But he who endures to the end shall be saved. And this gospel of the kingdom will be preached in all the

> world as a witness to all the nations,
> and then the end will come.
>
> Mathew 24:3-14 (NKJV)

The preaching of the gospel of the kingdom in all the world is not going to take long from today for the end to come but still Jesus Christ explained that no one knows the hour or time, so let us ready ourselves. Thanks to God, you had an opportunity to accept forgiveness in your confession in the past chapter.

In Matthew 24:7, Jesus gives the signs as follows: "For nation shall rise against nation, and kingdom against kingdom: and there shall be famines, and pestilences, and earthquakes, in diverse places."

These are the real times talked about by Jesus: nations are rising against nations, and kingdoms against kingdoms. Famine is everywhere today, and earthquakes are happening one after the other. People are losing their loved ones, their property, and there is such panic everywhere, and in this the devil plans that soon we shall lose focus from him, the enemy, and turn to blame ourselves, if possible, blame our neighbor, or even turn and blame God.

Yet, in all this, Jesus Christ taught so that we could be able to follow as events unfold, patiently waiting for salvation from the LORD God.

Jesus continues to speak about what will come next in Matthew 24:9 (NKJV): "Then shall they deliver you up to be afflicted, and shall kill you, and ye shall be hated of all nations for my name's sake."

When Jesus says; "they will deliver you," he is talking to believers. It's the believers who will be delivered up to be afflicted and shall be killed, and believers that will be hated of all nations for Jesus' sake. Fear will intensify so that believers will be silent about their faith in Jesus Christ. He says this so that we shall have courage to know that when all this happens he knows and sees what we shall be going through because he is the one telling this to us before it happens to us and it has happened to some of us already. Because such is happening to many in different countries.

He continues about those last days and says, "And then shall many be offended, and shall betray one another, and shall hate one another" (Matthew 24:10, NKJV).

Many shall be offended by the afflictions of the enemy in those days, so that some will have doubts.

If you have decided to follow Jesus Christ, his grace will abound upon us to take us through, for these things are not far from happening. In fact, such has begun already, and many have been offended already by what is going on all around us. God is in control. That's why Jesus Christ spoke about these things. So when they happen, as an individual, as a family, as a community, we must be careful always praying for salvation.

Our focus on the Prize everlasting life in heaven should not change because of the worry and despair and anger which will come into our hearts. This anger has got several intentions by the devil. Anger is not from God but from the devil. Jesus spoke about all of this so that we don't get offended when such things happen. Remember, you have given your life to Jesus Christ. "Let the body and the things of this world perish, yet your soul, will have everlasting life, because you have decided to trust in the LORD Jesus Christ" (Matthew 12:4-5, NKJV).

"And I say to you, My friends, do not be afraid of those who kill the body, and after that have no more that they can do. But I will show you whom you should fear: Fear Him who, after He has killed, has power to cast into hell; yes, I say to you, fear Him!" Matthew is talking about God.

Through the Scripture Jesus Christ added to what he had said saying, "...And many false prophets will rise and shall deceive many" (Matthew 24:11

NKJV). In deceptions, like turning many to forms of worship other than God the father, God the son, Jesus Christ, and God the Holy spirit, they, the false prophets, will stand as being sent from God, prophesying falsely and saying there are other ways for salvation other than through the LORD Jesus Christ and some calling them selves the Christ.

The devil plans to use the same reasoning when he, the antichrist, himself stands up to challenge us about our trust in Jesus Christ. He will use questions to let God look bad, pretending to be good as the hope of the world, promising to supposedly change things. Remember, he is causing today's damage already, and thereafter he will come to seemingly rectify the situation.

If God stays at the center of our lives, it will be very hard for the coming of the antichrist, because he won't find the world confused. So he will have no excuse to rule. The secret is that if the American people abide in serving God, staying focused to the purpose by helping those in need all round the world, as you have done, then the antichrist will find a hard landing. He will find no complaint about Jesus Christ, and the opposite is true if confusion, wars, divisions, and all sorts of evil abounds.

"And because iniquity shall abound, the love of many shall wax cold" (Matthew 24:12).

This prepares our hearts to even love more. We can notice that loving is a choice. God commands us to love, and it is, at times, very hard because of the way we love the things in the world. He says that, "He who shall endure in love unto the end, the same shall be saved." Enduring to the end will mean making choices to stay in the grace we received and in the love of God.

There will be times to test our faith and our commitment to Jesus. For example, with the choice you have made about following Jesus Christ as your Lord, some people will not believe you when you tell them about your decision to follow Jesus Christ. These can be at your place of work, some in your family and friends. Do not despair. It's good that you shall tell them and, more especially, the changed life that will manifest in you will prove your decision to follow Jesus Christ.

The future of America is to stand prepared for these bad times; to serve God with sincere hearts in these times and to resist the antichrist, who will rise in these times because of confusion, lack, and the many causes seen above.

This is why the devil purposefully wants the American people to be divided about the very issues that form our freedom. He plans to cause chaos among us. Remember, the devil is a respecter of no man. He tempted Jesus Christ, the Son of God, in the wilderness (Matthew 4:1). He has plans of continuing to tempt and use anyone, especially those in all kinds of authority.

Webster said:

> Let it be impressed on your mind that God commands you to choose for rulers just men who will rule in the fear of God [Exodus 18:21]… If the citizens neglect their duty and place unprincipled men in office, the government will soon be corrupted… If our government fails to secure public prosperity and happiness, it must be because the citizens neglect the Divine commands, and elect bad men to make and administer the laws.[14]

With all his knowledge, he advises us to stand united, with no division of religion, race, origins, rich, or poor and party. The enemy has attacked this land, and he is not restrictive of who he can use to achieve this objective. So watch, pointing fingers at each other will divide us, the community and nation, because division is not from God.

Remember, God will choose the faithful from the ones that served for wrong motives in the testing of our works which we have done here on earth. Let us then be pure to help each other to know God and agree to change from beliefs and values that are the basis of our divisions if our goal is to go to heaven. We need to check our motives for the need of control, need for power, positions, authority, and why we say we want to serve the country and God. God spoke through Paul to the Corinthian brethren the same way he speaks to the church in America today.

> Grace to you and peace from God our Father and the LORD Jesus Christ.
>
> I thank my God always concerning you for the grace of God which was given to you by Christ Jesus, that you were enriched in everything by Him in all utterance and all knowledge,

even as the testimony of Christ was confirmed in you, so that you come short in no gift, eagerly waiting for the revelation of our LORD Jesus Christ, who will also confirm you to the end, that you may be blameless in the day of our LORD Jesus Christ. God is faithful, by whom you were called into the fellowship of His Son, Jesus Christ our LORD.

Now I plead with you, brethren, by the name of our LORD Jesus Christ, that you all speak the same thing, and that there be no divisions among you, but that you be perfectly joined together in the same mind and in the same judgment. For it has been declared to me concerning you, my brethren, by those of Chloe's household, that there are contentions among you. Now I say this that each of you says, "I am of Paul, or I am of Apollos," or "I am of Cephas," or "I am of Christ." Is Christ divided?

1 Corinthians 1:3-23(NKJV)

These are the words of God by Paul to church but can very well help those in government, organizations, and as a nation. The intentions of God are to heal the willing and restore love and joy among us. He is holy; thus we must remain holy, without which none will see God.

"Follow peace with all [men], and holiness, without which no man shall see the LORD" (Hebrews 12:14, NKJV).

Wait not in fear, for these times and challenges are to come all over the world. Then if this is the future of America and the world, We have to remain in God's purpose and prepare for the antichrists, then judges, presidents, senators, representatives, teachers, apostles, preachers, evangelists, CEOs, supervisors, parents, leaders, fathers, and mothers, all with one goal, should be prepared to resist the devil so that he will flee from the Land. We have authority given to us by Jesus to do this. "And I will give you the keys of the kingdom of heaven, and whatever you bind on earth will be bound in heaven, and whatever you loose on earth will be loosed[d] in heaven" (Matthew 16:19 NKJV).

After he promised he then gave authority as we shall read ahead.

In our communities, we must be loving enough to tell the truth about our faith when opportunity strikes. Without confrontations guiding people into truth, we must help the ones that have fallen away from God by telling them what they do is wrong. We can't call this judging others, Jesus Christ himself the son of God said all and more of what we have read in this entire message yet he did not judge any one, he taught the word to show us how we can correct our wrong and if we don't believe in him then the word will judge us.

> And if anyone hears My words and does not believe, I do not judge him; for I did not come to judge the world but to save the world. He who rejects Me, and does not receive My words, has that which judges him—the word that I have spoken will judge him in the last day. For I have not spoken on My own authority; but the Father who sent Me gave Me a command, what I should say and what I should speak. And I know that His command is everlasting life.

> Therefore, whatever I speak, just as the Father has told Me, so I speak.
>
> John 12:47-50 (NKJV)

What God requires of us is to teach all things as he commanded us.

> And Jesus came and spoke to them, saying, "All authority has been given to Me in heaven and on earth. Go therefore[c] and make disciples of all the nations, baptizing them in the name of the Father and of the Son and of the Holy Spirit, teaching them to observe all things that I have commanded you; and lo, I am with you always, even to the end of the age." Amen.
>
> Matthew 28:18-20 (NKJV)

Following a command can't be called judging others when we speak the truth. This is the only way God will help through His Word. Let us prepare our hearts, because Jesus Christ is coming back. The times talked about in the Scriptures we have studied are these exact time. Let us believe and wait, praying salvation from Jesus Christ for all to believe.

Jesus Christ promised in John 16:23-24 And in that day you will ask Me nothing. Most assuredly, I say to you, whatever you ask the Father in My name, He will give you. Until now you have asked nothing in My name. Ask, and you will receive, that your joy may be full.

Please, let us ask God through Jesus Christ's name. He desires that we be joyful as we patiently do His will.

James Madison, fourth president of the United States, wrote,

> I have sometimes thought there could not be a stronger testimony in favor of religion or against temporal enjoyments, even the most rational and manly, than for men who occupy the most honorable and gainful departments and [who] are rising in reputation and wealth, publicly to declare the unsatisfactoriness [of temporal enjoyments] by becoming

> fervent advocates in the cause of Christ; and I wish you may give in your evidence in this way.[15]

When you read the president's writing above, be certain of one thing: that's his faith, has a sense of responsibility in this message; better than compromise. The responsibility is to teach the people and show them the way they should go, not to compromise for such cheap gains. Otherwise, we have failed if we don't tell the truth.

The forefathers created an atmosphere that welcomed the presence of God, because of their actions of faith and confessions. This was done not only in churches, but everywhere.

Thomas Jefferson said: "Of all the systems of morality, ancient or modern which have come under my observation, none appears to me so pure as that of Jesus."

George Washington, who served as the first President of the United States, said in his farewell address: "The name of American, which belongs to you, in your national capacity, must always exalt the just pride of Patriotism, more than any appellation derived from local discriminations. With slight shades of difference, you have the same religion… reason and experience both forbid us to expect, that national morality can prevail in exclusion of religious principle…"[16]

As a leader, he showed no doubt of where his stand was about religion. He showed the people the way because he was trusted when given this power and responsibility by the people. Government can be part of spreading this truth and to remind the people that this is not talking about just anything, but about God; the one who knows our tomorrow. Who else does?

James McHenry, an early American statesman and a signer of the United States Constitution from Maryland, said:

> Public utility pleads most forcibly for the general distribution of the Holy Scriptures. The doctrine they preach, the obligations they impose, the punishment they threaten, the rewards they promise, the stamp and image of divinity they bear, which produces a conviction of their truths, can alone secure to society, order and

> peace, and to our courts of justice and constitutions of government, purity, stability and usefulness. In vain, without the Bible, we increase penal laws and draw entrenchments around our institutions. Bibles are strong entrenchments. Where they abound, men cannot pursue wicked courses, and at the same time enjoy quiet conscience.

This observation has been the cornerstone for all this success. Without this, we have invited chaos. For example, when we were young, we were told why we had to brush our teeth in morning and after eating, although we wanted to eat without brushing first in the morning or sleep or run to play instead of brushing after eating. The problem was that we couldn't understand the consequences of not brushing, though our parents did.

This is the exact responsibility of government with the quote "God Bless America," because government has been around for many decades. Government knows why Jesus Christ is important so cannot stay silent about what the forefathers specifically did and why they did it, especially all the presidents we have seen.

On July 4, 1821, John Quincy Adams, the sixth president of the United States declared:

"The highest glory of the American Revolution was this; it connected in one indissoluble bond the principles of civil government with the principles of Christianity."

"From the day of the Declaration ... they (the American people) were bound by the laws of God, which they all, and by the laws of The Gospel, which they nearly all, acknowledge as the rules of their conduct." [17]

Benjamin Franklin was sixth President of the Supreme Executive Council of Pennsylvania. In his office 1749 plan of education for public schools in Pennsylvania, he insisted that schools teach "the excellence of the Christian religion above all others, ancient or modern."

Then in 1787, when Franklin helped found Benjamin Franklin University, it was dedicated as "a nursery of religion and learning, built on Christ, the Cornerstone."

This explains why government is to be at the center of preserving and protecting the Word of

God, supporting initiatives that have long before been supported to extend the great kingdom of Jesus Christ the LORD. After all we have read we can strongly stand to support the forefathers' initiatives, for example, the teaching of the Bible in our schools. Government should care about its people so much that it can guide us from history why this nation has stood for all these times.

We live in a free world, but government has its grounds which should not be shaken. Because which man, which system, which rule could give this freedom? Man can be so greedy that he can decide to change everything to suit his lusts, no matter what the cost, man looks for present gains and has little care and concern about tomorrow.

If we have honored the forefathers all these years, then it's wise that we consider why they are important: most importantly their faith in God. Despite what others will say about Jesus Christ the solid rock, he is the only hope for the nation, without whom the nation is on sinking sand.

Government (the people) should advise its citizens (ourselves) about the dangers of living a disobedient life. This was the whole intention of leadership from the beginning, as it was done by the previous leaders mentioned above.

This is God's advice to us, the American people, that restrictions be put off His Word, the Bible. How shall we stay free if the source of true freedom is not told to the people? This will be a sign to God for a changing nation. God is waiting to see this happen. Thanks to God for the systems and the avenues we have in place to change or improve issues. God sees and knows, and his plans never change, for his plans are to give America a good and peaceful life for our survival as He plans it for the whole world too. God bless America and God save America.

Blessed be the living word of God.

ENDNOTES

1 (Excerpts are inscribed on the walls of the Jefferson Memorial in the nation's capital)

2 In the Last Will and Testament of Patrick Henry [May 1765 Speech to the House of Burgesses]

3 The Mayflower Compact (authored by William Bradford) 1620 | Signing of the Mayflower painting | Picture of Compact69

4 The Principle approach by Rosalie Slater] pp.241-242 in Teaching and Learning America's Christian History

5 Constitutional Convention, Thursday' June 28, 1787

6 Constitutional Convention of 1787 original manuscript of this speech

7 John Adams in a letter written to Abigail on the day the Declaration was approved by Congress [April 18, 1775]

8 [1787 after the Constitutional Convention]

9 A Century of Lawmaking for a New Nation: U.S. Congressional Documents and Debates, 1774-1875 vol. vi, page 116 (12th Congress, 2nd Session Library of congress.)

10 Jefferson's Notes on the State of Virginia, Query XVIII, 1781(library of Congress)

11 1778 to the General Assembly of the State of Virginia

12 1828, in the preface to his American Dictionary of the English Language

13 Letters of Benjamin Rush, "To the citizens of Philadelphia: A Plan for Free Schools," March 28, 1787

14 Noah Webster, The History of the United States

15 Letter by Madison to William Bradford (September 25, 1773)

16 George Washington Papers at the Library of Congress, 1741-1799: Series 2 Letter books George Washington, September 17, 1796, Farewell Address

17 Speech of John Quincy Adams on July 4, 1821